SOME SOLDIER!

Some Soldier!
Adventures in the Desert War

by

Douglas Walter

PUBLISHED IN 1989
BY LINDEN HALL
223 PRESTON ROAD, YEOVIL,
SOMERSET BA20 2EW

© 1989 DOUGLAS WALTER

ISBN 0-948747-05-6
COVER DESIGN BY W. CAMERON JOHNSON
PRINTED IN MALTA BY INTERPRINT

Contents

1	Call-Up	13
2	We're in the Army Now!	18
3	'Up the Blue'	31
4	Lost and Found	37
5	Back to Tobruk, in a Hurry!	47
6	On my Own	54
7	'Caged'	60
8	Transit Camps	68
9	Italy	74
10	Campo Concentramento PG 70	80
11	Camp Industry	87

12	The Drama Group	91
13	My Name is Called Out!	96
14	The Way Back	100
15	Convalescent Leave	107
16	Despatch Rider	112
17	De-mob 'Daze'	118

Publisher's Preface

As a sailor who was at sea for the whole of World War II, sometimes calling into North Africa with stores for the Allied troops, before Montgomery arrived, I often wondered what life must have been like for the ordinary 'Tommy': stuck in the desert, being bombed and shelled.

Douglas Walter tells his personal story with wit, a wry humour and depth which helped me to understand how he and many others found the guts and fortitude to stick it out.

They were completely out-gunned and constantly retreating in front of Rommel's army, who were determined to capture Egypt and the oil fields beyond — without which it was most unlikely Europe could be conquered.

Douglas is a man small in stature but large in heart and humour. I found this book very hard to put down.

Captain Denis Foss
Merchant Navy

ST ALBANS, HERTFORDSHIRE

4th August 1989

As a raw subaltern these fifty years ago, I was approached by Driver D. C. Walter who was responding to my request for a new batman.

'In a time of quiet two days ago,' he said, 'I had the thought, "Look after Mr Ward." '

I soon realised that this little fellow was for me, and how grateful I was on many occasions that I had God and Doug at my side at the same time.

This book is quite a remarkable account of happenings and I wish it the greatest success.

Michael Newling Ward

1

Call-Up

I was called up in 1940. I went for my medical test and was passed A1 except for a slight deafness in my right ear, a family failing. This led to my being put in the Royal Army Service Corps.

When the time came, I joined my training depot at Inkerman Barracks, St John's, Woking. These barracks had been through some strange metamorphoses. The buildings started off, I believe, for prisoners from the Napoleonic wars, then they became a workhouse and now a barracks. There were certainly no home comforts there.

On arrival, I said cheerfully that I could ride a motorbike and would like to do despatch riding. What I'd forgotten, or rather not allowed for, was that the only motorbike I'd ever ridden, and that years previously, was my father's old-fashioned, quite small, and definitely old, Royal Enfield, the model that had a handle on the tank to move in a half-circle to change gear! The mechanical advances and changes between that old fellow and the seeming army giants (only 350 and 500cc actually) were stepping from one world into another and no mistake!

Twist grips for acceleration, foot gear changes and, of course, the size!

I was put on a course, and it was the most hair-raising fortnight of my life. Some mornings there were ice patches on the roads, but no matter, out we went. The first morning we were all experimenting, it seemed, how to start, how to get into gear. One fellow got into gear alright, but had no idea what to do next and slowly but surely moved off straight into a privet hedge, which fortunately stopped him.

The extreme of fear came the morning we were taken, like a flock of motorised sheep, all over the road, three or four abreast, some overtaking, some too slow and getting in the way, along to the famous Stony Castle on Camberley Heath. This was one of the obstacles on what was once a civilian test course for motor cycle scrambles. It was a terrifyingly steep hill with a loose six inch deep gravel and dirt surface, still further complicated by a wide, deep ditch or dyke which effectively stopped you getting up any real speed. The important thing about fear, I suppose, is first, don't show it and second, don't let it stop you.

Well, I'm not one of those to choose dangerous jobs for fun, and although I'd always had a head for heights and was fairly sure-footed, this wasn't my idea for thrills or for showing-off. However, up I had to go. Halfway my engine stalled, and from having to go straight up, I had somehow to turn round and come helter-skelter down the vertical face. This was even more frightening than going up, but I reached the level safely, heaved a great sigh of relief and thanksgiving, and went and told the instructor that

With the compliments of

GROSVENOR BOOKS
54 Lyford Road · London SW18 3JJ
Telephone 01-870 2124

Further copies £2.95 + 40p P+P

the bike wasn't powerful enough. Promptly, he replied, 'OK, take mine, it's a 500cc.'

So, off I had to go again — into the ditch and then full blast up the hill, skidding and sliding, until at the top I literally took off with my own velocity. Sizing up the lie of the land as quickly as I could, I turned and made my way down the laughingly called 'safe' route! I don't think I ever stopped praying during the course. Even on the roads there were so many others round you, you couldn't feel safe. I longed for a solo run, just to practise in my own time.

Having survived and passed out successfully, in time-honoured Army fashion, I didn't get to a motorbike again, until after my repatriation from a POW camp, in Italy, about two years later.

All this time, we were having lessons on how to drive the 'Army' way in trucks and lorries: double-declutching, both up and down gears, night driving in the blackout, both hands on the wheel. We were taught to forget our so-called 'bad' civilian habits. We also had shooting practice and map-reading lectures.

These afforded light relief after the hair-raising motorbikes, although at Bisley, when we went for our passing-out tests, I suddenly got an insane idea that the bolt of the rifle, when I pulled the trigger, was going to come back and hit me in the eye instead of forward to fire the bullet. Because of this irrational panic, my first shot went right off target, but with a quick prayer the fear went and all the other shots were nicely grouped near the centre. I passed these tests, in spite of all my tensions and fears.

Guard duty was another kind of nightmare. As well as all the 'bull' of getting ready and being inspected, then the elaborate performance of the changing of the guard, there was also the very real possibility of falling asleep on duty and being caught by the occasional inspection. Because of my deafness, I might not hear anyone coming and a court martial, if found sleeping, would have been inevitable. I don't think I would have been shot if this had happened, but deafness would not have been an acceptable excuse.

There was a square-sided tower at these barracks and it took four of us, one at each side at the top, to keep watch, like so many bowmen on the battlements of some mediaeval castle. I can only suppose we were plane-spotters or fire-watchers. We were never told. One compensation about certain guard points, at night especially, was their very quietness. I could revel in the blacked-out landscape, the moonlight, the stars and silence.

One morning on a day when I was due to go on duty that night up the tower, I had the thought, 'Do not withdraw, but talk to someone.' I didn't welcome the thought. It was against my inclination. But it went back to an unusual experience I had had before joining up. At the prompting of some friends I had met in the Oxford Group (now known as Moral Re-Armament: MRA), I had decided to get up earlier than my usual last-minute rush every day and in a time of quiet discover whether God could give me guidance for my life. I'd been bothered by some personal matters so I made this promise to God in the faith that something would happen. I'd made a start in 'civvy street' and found that the practical thoughts I got in the mornings were a great help. Nevertheless

I was a bit apprehensive of what God might tell me to do in the less congenial atmosphere of the army.

So I wasn't particularly pleased when I got the idea to talk to someone on duty. 'Oh dear', I thought, 'bang go my quiet two hours!' I decided to talk to the fellow guardsman who had been in the Salvation Army. He'd be sure to agree with my ideas even if not with my way of expressing them, then I'd get a bit of peace.

It worked out alright, except that next morning the guard from the far side of the tower came up to me and said he couldn't help overhearing what I had been saying to the Salvationist about my decision to change and let God run my life, the things I had had to put right, and about God's forgiveness and His daily, continuing direction; please, would it work for him? We found a quiet room in the guard-house, talked, and then kneeling down together, he gave his life to God and started off to live a new way.

This was a great encouragement. God was at work even in these unpromising conditions.

We were at the barracks for some two or three months. We all looked forward to our passing-out parade most eagerly and to being posted to our permanent units and getting settled.

Posting came eventually, but as for getting settled — nothing could be further from the truth.

2

We're in the Army Now

A number of us were posted to No 1 Ambulance Car Company at Bradford. We were billeted in empty houses, sleeping on the floor on palliasses (called 'biscuits', for some undiscovered reason) and eating our meals in a school building a few miles up the road. All this in the coldest winter ever, it seemed, with snow everywhere, piled up at the sides of the roads.

We would be taken up to meals in the back of a lorry, and it never failed to amuse me the way the men would spill out when the tail flap was lowered on our arrival, all spontaneously baaing and bleating like sheep! This probably helped us to overlook the way we *were* being treated — like sheep!

As I cycled along a country lane one day, I suddenly realised the full implications of what had happened to me. Before the war started I was the Display Manager at a family store in Slough, Buckinghamshire, where I had a comfortable flat. Being only 5 ft 5 in, my shortness was quite an advantage in my work. My name was probably less important now than my army number, 228136. I'd left my flat and all my civilian clothes behind. I was completely dispossessed of all I had, in one sense.

Then the realisation came, not that I was without anything, but that everything, all England, the whole world was mine. I was responsible, and I was able to feel that I was fighting for them morally and spiritually, as well as physically. It was a revealing experience which I have never forgotten.

We were issued with the most soul-destroying tropical kit you ever saw. Old-fashioned topees (Boer War, I should think), long shorts that turned up and were buttoned in big bags round your knees, to be let down at night to keep off the mosquitoes, and heavy army boots, to complete the picture. We couldn't wait to try everything on, and after the first hysterical reaction, several of us took the kit into Bradford to be photographed in.

Eventually we boarded *The Empress of Canada* at Gourock, and after an interminable wait finally set sail. Our sleeping quarters were way, way down below decks. When our many hammocks were slung, with the strings at head and feet overlapping, we were so crowded that the effect was for all the world like being up in the branches of a forest of grey, dead palm trees. Underneath us, on the floor, were some huge, ominous-looking bins, reaching nearly to chest height. Surely not for litter? I think, even before we reached the Bay of Biscay, we knew exactly what they were for! Nearly everyone seemed to be seasick, including me. Curiously, I wasn't actually sick but I couldn't eat a thing for three days, and I spent my time lying flat on a damp deck, dizzy, cold and utterly miserable.

Soon the weather picked up, we began to find our sea-legs, and a new battle began, to find a space on deck for sleeping. At first this was no great problem and it eased the overcrowding down in the hold. Then everyone cottoned on to the idea of tropical nights sleeping under the stars, with the ship's masts moving gently overhead.

When we reached Freetown we hove to, but we weren't allowed ashore in spite of all our inoculations, for fear of fever. What a wonderful sight it was! Truly golden yellow sands, with sugarloaf hills covered with dark green palm trees, and perhaps most exciting of all, after the blackout in England and at sea, at night there were shore lights blazing and car lights snaking up the steep hills. It was breathtakingly lovely.

Soon we were on our way again, blacked-out, of course, but getting warmer all the time. Amongst other things, I volunteered to do a water course, on how to make drains and soakaways etc. Then confirmation classes were started by the Church of England padre. I was born and brought up a Congregational non-conformist, but went to a Roman Catholic Convent kindergarten. A Methodist introduced me to the reality of the Christian life and MRA. A fairly ecumenical beginning. However, I thought the classes might be reasonably cultural, and interesting folk might be there.

Before we completed the course we were landed at Port Tewfik and carted off to a tented camp in the desert to acclimatise. This camp was near Ismailia and the sweet water canal, which was anything but sweet. The Assistant Bishop of Egypt was going to be in the district for some days, and he gave us a special dispensation to be confirmed if we wanted to, in spite of our incomplete instruction. So, anything to get even a day away from this awful camp and into a town, I put my name down. Not the best of reasons for getting confirmed, I daresay, but it did stick.

I go too fast. Before we got to Egypt, there was a brief stop at Cape Town. What an extraordinary experience that was. Every day it seemed as if the whole city lined up in cars at the docks, and these wonderful South Africans took charge of parties of delighted soldiers. They gave them rides, money, cigarettes, meals and, above all, a sincere and warm welcome. There were the lights, flowers, shops filled with good things, and no rationing!

I got a telephone number from an MRA poster on the dockside, and quite miraculously met up with friends I knew in England. They managed to get hold of a car and belted me round Table Mountain by day, then in the evenings I was taken to hastily convened gatherings where I told them of life in blacked-out Britain, especially in London.

Back to the ship and on again, up through the Red Sea to Port Tewfik. On land once more and humping our baggage, we were shunted to our tented, desert camp for acclimatising. I think we were there for about two months.

My trip into Ismailia for my confirmation was a stunning experience, after all the time in the dry, dusty desert, suddenly to find flame trees with their vivid green foliage, blazing in full bloom with their scarlet flowers beside the Canal; green, watered lawns around them and, or course, authentic work-

21

ing camels and pukka Arabs leading them. They all seemed to be carrying water melons, but perhaps it was just harvest time for these.

One other trip out from the camp I had during this time, was to go into town and collect up a biggish lorry and take it, by myself, to Port Said, pick up a naval officer and all his furniture and personal belongings, and take him miles by the desert road to Cairo! I was very scared, not least by the fact that it was taken for granted that I *could* drive that sort of lorry, and *could* find my way. I picked up the lorry, and apart from driving off, after all the warnings, on the wrong, left hand side of the road (from excitement and force of habit), all went well.

All went well, that is, except that the naval type I was picking up seemed deeply to resent being posted and sulked and just wouldn't talk to me, with the result that on the long, hot, melting tarmac road across the featureless desert, I fell asleep and suddenly left the road with a mighty lurch. This woke us both up! Fortunately, I kept my head and kept my foot down on the accelerator, kept moving in the loose sand, and in a great, circular sweep round, I got the lorry back on the road. There was much swearing and recrimination until I heatedly pointed out that if only he'd chatted to me a bit, I wouldn't have fallen asleep. After that, he did try, not very successfully though.

On our arrival at his destination in Cairo, he got off the lorry without a word. Naval men came out and unloaded his stuff, and there I was, without any further instructions, without a bed for the night, and very far from home!

I somehow found, of all places, the Military Police Barracks at Kom-el-Dik in the city, a one-time fort of Napoleon's. Here I made up a bed in the back of my lorry, and in the morning, I queued up with the military police types for breakfast, all without a query or a word being said. No check was made. It could have been a normal, overnight procedure. They had a tame lamb there, just wandering around, which they used to feed on scraps, very like a pet dog. Sometime later, when I went back there, the lamb had become a sheep and was considerably less endearing, and much more of a nuisance!

Our next move was into tents in the grounds of the Mohammed Ali Barracks, in Alexandria. In the city, I was able to find a team of mixed nationalities united together to bring MRA as an active force into the lives of their families, their friends, and their nations. These folk were varied, some very rich, some their servants, some students. They included a Swiss cotton planter, two university professors, a Russian, an Austrian-Swiss family, some Sudanese, an English lady who ran a College for Social Service Studies. They were an oasis of open-hearted hospitality, civilised living, and a demonstration to me of how nations could unite for a common aim and purpose which was big enough and unselfish enough.

Back in England, a sergeant and a corporal had seemed to take a dislike to me (or perhaps it was for what they suspected I stood for), and went out of their way to catch me if I came in a few minutes late accidentally, or some other thing that seemed trivial to me. The sergeant was now going to have his opportunity in Alexandria. Quite reprehensibly, I got rather tired of reading 'Standing Orders' every day. For one thing they never seemed to change.

Then, one day, the inevitable happened. There was a full moon and they ordered us into barracks at night a little earlier than usual, possibly to avoid air raids. Not having read these new orders, I arrived back at the barracks, not a quarter of an hour early, as I thought in all innocence, but half an hour late! This sergeant fellow had had great difficulty trying to find me, and when he did I was promptly put on a 'Charge'.

The next morning I had to go through the ignominious performance of being marched in at the double before the colonel, cap off, standing strictly to attention and feeling horribly guilty and foolish, even before the trial had started. I should think that, even worse than my 'lateness' crime, my defence that I'd not read standing orders that day was like committing sacrilege. I was formally found guilty and put on 'jankers'. This time confined to barracks for a week, and, incidentally, given rather lousy jobs to do — more than one's usual share of spud-bashing, for instance.

One of these jobs they thought up was to scrub out the colonel's office. Think of it. In that climate! Now, I had learnt that the way to overcome the tedium of boring or distasteful work is really to tackle it — to get all the 'eyes' out of the potatoes, for instance, and clean a thing thoroughly. I suppose this was just simple psychology, but now was the chance to apply a bit of inspired 'psychology'.

I decided I would *really* do the colonel's office. I moved all the furniture and filing cabinets to one side, and soon found myself sweating profusely, but, nevertheless, singing happily under my breath, scrubbing out some dirt in a corner, which seemed to have been there since the Pyramids were built. At this moment, in comes the colonel, apologises for disturbing me, asks permission to get something from his desk, and after I had given him leave tiptoes over the floor to the desk, then turns and tiptoes out again!

On another occasion, that same week, I was put on telephone duty for the evening. The telephone was in an L-shaped army hut, with the 'phone and office and I in one leg, and a kind of NCO's sitting room in the other. The sergeant and others were there, and I was quite pleasantly filling in time, reading a book.

Presently, I heard the sarge bemoaning the fact that he'd owed his wife a letter for three weeks, but he could not think of anything to say except: 'This lousy country; too hot, too dusty, too dirty, and so on.' I found out later, that they'd only been married three weeks, and he'd not known her much longer, before coming out to the Middle East, so, in a sense, they'd hardly got to know one another, let alone discover any common interests.

One could understand his feelings about the place — barracks in England are bad enough, artistically speaking, but out there the surroundings are drab, even allowing for a few 'art and crafty' palm trees in silhouette against the twilight sky, coupled with a couple or so mosques and minarets. Many of the houses, on the outskirts especially, seemed only half-completed, or falling down. Gardens were nonexistent, the ground not cultivated, rocky, dirty, dusty and dry. Willing though I was to appreciate everything, I had to work overtime on my artistic appreciation!

The grumbling went on until I suddenly heard another voice say, 'Walter is just round the corner, he's always writing letters. Why don't you ask him to write one for you?' To my amazement, the sergeant jumped at the idea and called out to me, 'Will you write a letter to my wife for me?' I replied 'Of course not, I don't know her.' He continued to press me, in spite of my telling him that he wouldn't write what I put down, so it would be a waste of time.

He promised he would, and I suddenly had an idea: I'd make the letter a 'confession' of all his faults and weaknesses as I saw them, with a promise to change, try to let God have a say in the running of his life, and become a proper person and part of the new world we were fighting for.

Well, I thought, that will at least tell him how he seems to those of us at the receiving end of his tempers, hangovers and bullying. All of which I included in the letter.

To my astonishment, he went into raptures over it, wrote it out word for word, admitting all the shortcomings and telling of his new desire to change, and promptly sent it off to his wife. He had a very quick reply, and needless to say, she was delighted with his decision.

Now, here was a dilemma — how did he follow it up? He asked me to write him another letter, but this time I very firmly refused, although I gave him a few basic ideas: about his slowness to change, and places where he could buck things up still more.

I offered him a very readable and amusing book called *Ideas Have Legs*, by Peter Howard, in which he tells of how his marriage was affected by his change. Here, however, I came across a curious phenomenon, which I have found with quite a few people. They'll listen to you talk about a book, or quote from a book, but there is often no desire to read it for themselves and directly absorb the ideas and philosophy. Perhaps it is a habit they have never been encouraged in or, perhaps just an inability to concentrate? I guess this is where visual aids are such a help in teaching.

After this taste of the big city we were detailed to go up to Palestine. So off we went, trailing in convoy, with our tuck wagon, ambulances, complete with 'bivvies' (bivouac tents), outriders on motor bikes, and the rest, to the Canal crossing at Kantara. Then the long drive north, occasionally relieving the monotony of the desert road by passing through or near villages or towns with well-known Biblical names which were, sadly, quite unlike the popular, traditional idea of Biblical villages.

They were hot and dusty, full of Palestinians who didn't seem particularly pleased to see us, or even to notice us; except for the street vendors with their endless cries of 'Eggs and bread', and the beggars asking for 'Baksheesh!'. At last, we passed through Nazareth which was very beautiful, being built on both sides of a deepish valley.

Our first base was at the Sarafand Barracks, near Tel-a-Viv. Here there were a camp cinema, avenues of eucalyptus trees and vineyards all round, with orange groves nearby. One lasting impression was a pump throbbing away constantly, audible for miles, presumably to bring up the life-giving water and make it available to the crops in the fields through a quite remarkable system of damming and undamming and re-damming a complex system of gutters dug into the sloping sides of the fields of crops. Here at Sarafand we also had beds and a fixed roof over our heads, which made a nice change.

One morning I was trying to lift my thinking above my purely personal problems and plans. I asked God how I, a very ordinary 'other' rank, could best help the well-being of my unit. The answer came back pat, and I wrote it down: 'Take care of Mr W...' He was the young lieutenant in charge of our detachment (our OC).

I couldn't see how I was going to carry out my order but two days later, right out of the blue, our sergeant came up to me and said that Mr W's batman wanted a change and would I like to 'take care of Mr W?'. I said at once, 'Yes, I would.' He took me along to the OC's tent and Mr W repeated the suggestion adding, on hearing my acceptance: 'Wouldn't you like to think it over?' So I showed him my notebook and the words I had written down two days before, and told him where I thought the idea had come from. He seemed a little taken aback, but didn't back down.

So began a very real friendship which went on until our capture by the Germans and resumed after the war was over. My OC came back from prison camp later than I, so I was able to contact his wife and father and assure them of his well-being. He and his

wife came to my wedding and we still exchange cards at Christmas.

The unit moved from Sarafand up to Haifa for a short spell. While we were there, he and I made a quick dash up to Damascus to check on one of our detachments near there. We didn't like Damascus very much. It was more or less under siege, or else in a mild state of civil war, so, after one or two shots were fired in our vicinity, we patted our outpost section on the back, wished them luck and got to hell out of it!

The desert the OC and I had to cross to get back to Haifa, the Syrian I suppose, seemed very bleak and unfriendly, stretching on for miles and swept by a hot dusty wind. We came to the River Jordan and eventually stopped for our midday rations beside Galilee.

We visited Jerusalem later, when my OC was invited to play in a cricket match there. This gave me a chance to have a wander round, although everywhere you went, you came up against 'Out of Bounds' signs. There was an atmosphere of general objection and antagonism to the British being there. It was plainly not safe to move around too much.

While we were at Haifa an incident took place which had interesting repercussions for me later on. One of our bunch was caught flogging rifles to some Arabs and was put under close arrest. Shortly after this we were all shifted back to Alexandria (getting to seem like home to me, by now), leaving the culprit behind to be court-martialled. Not long after my OC and four or five of the other ranks were summoned back to Haifa as witnesses in this gun-runner's trial.

Our company was ordered off to the desert, but

much to my surprise, I was left behind in Alexandria to take care of my OC's truck. I was to be in nominal touch with the South African Battalion stationed there for my pay, meals and so on, but no parading or duties. One of the South African officers, noticing I didn't use the truck, told me I *must* use it, to keep the battery charged and, come to that, the sand blown off! So there I was for five weeks alone in this wonderful city, surrounded by hospitable friends and with free transport.

Soon after my OC's return from Haifa and my long 'vacation', we received our orders. We were to pack up and leave. We 'other ranks' were not told where we were going, or the route. This was probably for security reasons. All we had to go on was the sheer completeness of the move and, of course, plenty of rumours. These did little to offset the discomfort and feelings of uncertainty.

3

'Up the Blue'

It was very peculiar, this going up in to the desert, literally into the 'Blue'. We soon found out how the desert got its nickname; even the vast flat of the desert itself was dwarfed by the overwhelming, completely unbroken blue of the sky.

As my OC and I, with the witnesses from the trial up in Palestine, moved out of Alexandria along the road, the Army and RAF camps became fewer, the villages more intermittent, and then quite suddenly civilisation ended. Tracks branched off in all directions, some signposted in a half-hearted, jocular sort of way, as was done in World War 1, when the trenches were called after Piccadilly, Oxford Circus, and so on, but all of them leading to an absolutely featureless horizon. These tracks had been made by the Italians advancing and then the British driving them back. There seemed no meaning to them in terms of direction or use.

There was nothing except scrub, like heather but dried up and colourless, plain blue sky and these churned-up dirty, dusty tracks. It took your breath away. It was like looking at a dry, brown, motionless ocean. Its vastness was overwhelming. For once the soldier's favourite swear word seemed justified: 'miles and miles of ... all!' Hopefully, we believed our OC knew where we were going.

We stayed on the one road which runs along the top of that part of North Africa, not far from the Mediterranean but just out of sight, not that we knew that at the time. So it was all the more delighted surprise when we discovered that all the time we had been on a plateau. Suddenly the road went over the edge and dropped away down an almost sheer escarpment, hairpinning down to a fantastic, small white town nestling in the dark green palms, fronting on to dazzling white sands, and the most wonderful, sparkling, sapphire-blue sea.

When we eventually got down to the town, we found it completely deserted by its civilian population, and a great disappointment. This was Mersa Matruh. It had been, and was to become again, a popular and smart holiday resort for the Egyptians. At this time it was sadly knocked about, by naval bombardment, we thought.

We stayed the night here and then on, passing through or by deserted, shot-up seaside towns like Derna and Sidi-Barrani, and through Fort Capuzzo again shelled to absolute ruins. We were getting an almost superstitious respect for the guns of the Navy!

Down the sheer escarpment to Wadi Halfaya: there was very impressive road building on these precipitous slopes. Then on for mile after mile of dirty, dusty landscape without even the traditional sand dunes I'd always believed were an essential part of any self-respecting desert.

Gradually we began to catch up with where the action had been fought out a few days previously. There were shot-up and burnt-out planes and tanks. In some planes there were still bands of ammunition. We couldn't resist salvaging some for our own possible use in the future; what on, I don't know. We had seen a small, deer-like creature, not much bigger than a hare, on our way up, and that was about the extent of the wild life, except for the inevitable vultures (popularly known as shitehawks), the invaluable scavengers of camp and desert.

At last we came to El Adem, I think it was, although there was nothing to mark the spot, just slightly higher and with deeper undulations in the rocky environment. A seemingly, to me, quite pointless location. Here we rejoined our unit. I suppose our ambulances did go out on operations, transporting wounded from the field dressing posts to the next place down the line with more resources and facilities, but I didn't see much of this side of things, as I stayed by as the OC's driver and head cook and bottle washer.

All this time we were on very dull rations of interminable supplies of corned beef and army biscuits, occasionally with tinned vegetables to mix in to make a stew. As Christmas Day approached we began to think even more longingly of fresh meat and some sort of variety in the pudding line, and so we spent quite a lot of time scouting around trying to find the NAAFI supplies, or following up rumours of travelling YMCA or Red Cross 'comforts' vans.

On the Derna marshes bordering the sea we had spotted some wild ducks, and we decided that here could be our fresh meat supplies! Gathering up our newly acquired ammunition and rifles, and spurred on by the thought of roast duck for supper, we set off fairly stealthily, near enough down wind, and of course quite without any ridiculous ideas of sportingly starting the birds into flight. The more 'sitting' ducks the better as far as we were concerned. We wanted roast duck — badly! This was, it seemed to us, survival.

It was the first time since our training that most of us would have used our rifles. In fact, as we were attached to an ambulance unit, we shouldn't have had them anyway. We used to keep them wrapped up in a sheet or blanket to protect them against the dust and sandstorms, carefully hidden away under our kit. Out of sight and, except for a very occasional inspection, usually out of mind.

Down on the marsh I earmarked a possible victim, standing or floating on one of the big stretches of shallow sea-water on the beach. I crept as close as I dared, about 100 yards or maybe less, took careful aim, held my breath as per instructions, squeezed the trigger, and without stopping to think how I would retrieve the bird, I fired. Amazingly, I hit it — with an explosive bullet! The poor duck was shattered, and so was I. I found out afterwards, alas too late, that at intervals on these bands of bullets there would be an explosive bullet and it had been my bad luck to use one!

Everyone let off rapidly and of course all the birds for miles round were airborne and away. We did bag two or perhaps three. Well, alright, perhaps not roast duck for supper, but we could at least have duck stew. This idea was also a complete failure. The birds were so tough, salty and fishy, I don't think anyone was able to tackle them, or even the stew! Ah well, back to the bully beef.

After this fiasco, there was still the arduous task of pouring boiling water down the spout (or should I say, barrel) of your gun, pulling it through and generally restoring it to its 'clean, bright and oily' condition.

That was the end of our big game hunting. No more safaris for us. The inborn English prejudice that all foreign food was rotten, full of bacteria and generally inferior to the home-grown stuff, especially when it came to ducks, was once again fully endorsed!

Gradually we settled down to a routine which was altered as soon as we became familiar with it. No sooner had we worked out the quickest route to the nearest NAAFI supply depot than we would be ordered to move some miles away, to an equally arid and seemingly pointless location. As I've already said, the actual day's work of the ambulances as such passed me by. They would go off empty on a detail and having done their job of transporting wounded, would return in the evening, empty.

It was at this time that the Australian garrison which had held Tobruk for so long was relieved, and the British forces were sweeping forward rapidly. All the officers developed a craze for 'desert boots', buckskin, lace-up boots in sand colour, and very comfortable to wear and rather smart. I suppose the suede effect brought a touch of refinement and chic, even if they were not actually haute couture! One of my priorities came to be to get to the Tobruk stores, army of course, and buy a pair for my boss. I think they helped his morale, but, alas, they were not allowed for us 'other ranks'.

During these days up in the desert we had formed a foursome, an officer, Basil, from a nearby section, my OC, the platoon sergeant, Tony, and myself to play Bridge in the evenings, in one of the vehicles which my boss had made into his HQ and bed-sitter. You can tell the level of play; when, after a few months, I suggested we learnt how to play Contract Bridge, to make a change. They all turned on me and informed me that that was what we had been playing all the time!

The Army swept on with us, like camp followers, trailing on behind. We passed the famous 'Knightsbridge' box, a supposedly naturally defensive area, but which to my untutored, non-military mind looked exactly as vulnerable as anywhere else about there. Perhaps there were more strategic minefields around the area, with limited entrances and exits.

On towards Benghazi, and as we progressed the countryside began to look more interesting and quite hopeful until one day we climbed a steep escarpment, and there suddenly, Shangri-la! The climate and the character of the countryside completely changed: greenery everywhere and signs of cultivation. The quick transition from dirt and desert to delightful scenery and surroundings, was like magic, a miracle. The 'desert blossoming like the rose'! So, farewell Libya, Cyrenaica, hullo!

4

Lost and Found

During the long, hot days of the summer before we left the desert, we developed what was almost a routine. Every day the ambulances would go out on a detail, return and report. Then the damages to the vehicles would be checked over. Broken springs were the usual casualty and so next day off the ambulances would have to limp to a map reference quite a few miles away, where the mobile workshop/maintenance team had their temporary, tented quarters.

Now it was my turn. Our truck developed the inevitable spring trouble. At the repair camp the job could not be done right away, so I was to be left overnight to wait for it. 'Do you know the way back?' 'Yes, of course, I know', I replied. 'Quite sure?' 'Quite sure.'

It was wonderful to be away from continuous authority for a while, to be in a sense on my own. The next morning, in this repair camp, I had my usual quiet time. This was the time before starting the day's activities for a spot of prayer, perhaps a dip into my little pocket edition of Moffatt's translation of the New Testament, then the very important part, asking

God to help me plan the day ahead. I sought to direct my thinking as far as possible along the lines of what He wanted me to do and how, rather than just trusting to my own rather rocky judgement.

Two thoughts which I wrote down in my notebook stand out very clearly in my memory: 'If anyone is detailed to travel with you, be grateful.' The other thought: 'Be prepared to talk.' I liked being alone and quiet, and able to think.

I had been offered a map which I had refused on the grounds that I had forgotten how to read maps, and that there were no landmarks or other features, apart sometimes from a few empty petrol cans piled up or a few large stones or rocks in a line. Anyway, the route back to my unit seemed simple enough to my mind.

Sure enough, someone *was* detailed to come with me, a corporal who was being transferred from one unit to another, and our post would be on his way, also an ambulance and the driver. The corporal turned out to be my old 'friend' from the early army days back in England, who had put me on a charge of being late in one night! 'Be grateful, be prepared to talk!' This was certainly stretching me, but things were taken out of my hands completely when the corporal, who opted to ride with me, suddenly turned to me just after we'd started and said, quite unexpectedly, 'Well, how is MRA up in the desert, then?' I didn't even know he knew of my connection with it! 'Very well, thank you', I replied meekly.

There was to be no escaping. 'What is MRA exactly?' was the next question. So I took my courage in both hands, took a deep breath and launched out.

I told him of my making a decision to let God run my life; how I had used the four absolute standards of honesty, purity, unselfishness and love to check over my life. How I had written down the things that God told me had been wrong, to put right as He directed, and to ask for and accept forgiveness for the lot. I had then started to receive 'guidance' which I wrote down in my notebook in my morning time of early quiet: thoughts of how to tidy up my life and run it better, and thoughts of what God wanted me to do for Him to start bringing in a new world.

I gave some examples of how God's guidance works from my experience. One occasion was getting lost in thick fog on my way to an important interview with a colonel. The territory was relatively unknown to me. It was dark and cold. Crawling along the unfamiliar lanes was pretty hopeless, so I decided to stop and ask someone the way — that is, if there was someone! A figure loomed up in the fog: Yes, he knew where the colonel lived: 'This is his front gate!'

The corporal and I talked all the morning, he asking relevant questions and showing great interest. And then it happened! The next pile of stones or petrol cans didn't materialise, nor the next. I didn't even know which way we had come. We were well and truly lost.

My first reaction after the natural trepidation of what being lost in the desert could entail was, what would the corporal say? Would he turn round and suggest, albeit ever so sweetly, that I got some of this 'guidance' I'd been talking about so enthusiastically? It is quite one thing to report things that have happened through following thoughts that may or may not have come from God, but on being obeyed had had a miraculous and successful outcome in the relative security of 'civvy street', and quite another to ask for a route to safety.

All that afternoon as we wandered here and there, trying to find our way over this dry, dusty, flat and featureless landscape, I expected the inevitable question. But no, I think he must have got hold of the idea that you only got 'guidance' first thing in the morning.

We parked for the night and had our supper, warmed up over a petrol/sand fire in an old biscuit tin, and we began to turn in. Then began a curious, furious battle in me. Should I put God, or rather my faith, to this test and ask for guidance to find the way? I felt very strongly that if I said my prayers that night (and Heaven knows I needed to), I must logically have a quiet time of 'listening' in the morning!

I walked away from the trucks a little way. It was quite velvety dark with a vast sky of stars, and so still and quiet you could almost feel the silence. I committed myself. I told God I'd have a morning quiet time, and asked Him specially to be in it. As I prayed, I began to realise just why the prophets, the hermits, even Jesus himself, had retired to the desert so often. The stillness, silence and the sense of God's presence were terrific.

The next morning I got up early and made some tea for the three of us, them climbed into the front seat of the truck. As I sat there, with my notebook at the ready, but still as confused as ever by all the criss-crossing of tracks made by friends and foes alike, advancing and retreating, I gave up trying to reason out a route, and just said to God, 'Alright, I'll write down the first thought that comes.'

At that moment the sun rose quickly above the horizon in front of me and one track stood out, shadowed a little darker than the others, 'The track half left of east', I wrote down quickly. A great sense of relief came over me, that I had been able to write down something. Right or wrong? These tracks were just ruts rather than tracks, really!

As I wrote the words down, a knock came behind me and the corporal's voice said, 'Are you having the usual?' My heart sank as I replied, 'Yes!' 'Good', he said.

We had our breakfast, and the three of us stood in a circle to confer, the corporal looking at me expectantly: 'Well, which way do we go, then?' As he said it, he winked at me knowingly, as if to say, '*We* know where you've got the direction from, don't we?' This was terrible! However, I pointed out the track I'd had indicated (as I hoped), and said: 'That one'. The other driver disagreed. He wanted to take the almost opposite direction. This, we found out later, would have taken us to the enemy-occupied coast. The corporal plumped for what I'd written down, and so we packed up and set off.

That very same track took us straight back to camp! After seventy-two miles, to my intense relief, I suddenly realised we were driving between two rows of casually spaced petrol cans indicating the way in. The corporal turned to me and said, 'Well, that's a bloody miracle! That's converted me!'

From what I heard later, it really seems it had!

From being a disgruntled, disruptive cuss in whatever unit he happened to be, from insisting on over-discipline and arbitrary work details, all additionally irritating to men in dodgy surroundings and circumstances, he became helpful and encouraging.

We were mighty thankful to be safe back in the repair camp, even though it wasn't our own base. That evening in the big leisure marquee we were all given a bonus letter form so that we could write an extra letter home for Christmas. These forms were for micro-filming to save space on the mail planes and enlarging back in England.

I was happily stuck in reporting the news of the hair-raising excitements of the last two days, when I heard the sergeant-major, a complete stranger, virtually, call out across the crowded tent: 'Hey, Walter, tell us about MRA!' This was something I hadn't bargained for: to be called on to get up and in cold blood make an impromptu speech to a bunch of rough, tough guys I didn't know, so I quickly replied, 'Oh, you wouldn't understand,' and carried on writing. After a short silence, his voice came again, 'Come on, we're all waiting!'

Well, what was I to do? I certainly mustn't preach, give 'em too much challenge and put them off, or even not enough challenge and lose them? There was no time for preparation. I prayed frantically: 'Help!' And then the thought came clearly, 'Don't try to be clever, give news, not views, just talk, don't make a speech!'

So I did just that. I decided to speak from my heart, just as it came. I told them about the four absolute moral standards which were a kind of condensation of the Sermon on the Mount, and could be used as a yardstick to measure our lives against, and then make restitution for anything that didn't measure up: repair the radio, so to speak, so that we could 'listen in', be guided by God, whatever we did, wherever we were. I ended up with the hot news of getting lost the day before, of asking for direction, writing it down, and so being guided back to safety!

The immediate effect was quite spontaneous and almost amusing. Everybody started being 'unselfish', quite remarkably noticeable. They all began offering each other their rationed cigarettes (like gold dust, these were). 'Have a cigarette?' 'No, no, you have one of mine' and so on. It was most interesting.

A couple of days later my OC came to collect me. Just as we were driving away, the sergeant-major came running up, and said to my OC, 'Can't you leave him here a bit longer? That evening was the most interesting we've had since we've been up in the desert. The whole unit has been working as a team, and even the two lazy buggers are pulling their weight!' I don't remember what my OC said in reply, but I remember there were no recriminations over my original over-confidence in myself as a route finder.

Before we go any further, there is one other story of getting lost in the desert I must tell. It happened on our first day coming up. During the afternoon, after we had got over the initial shock of seeing this appalling wilderness of a desert in all its grimness, we found we had to strike off the road for some reason and follow a track which quickly degenerated into mere tyre marks, and eventually into a mere confusion of nothing!

We found we were quite lost, and I expect we panicked a bit. My OC, who was driving, began to go faster and to everyone's discomfort seemed to go straight at every lump, bump or depression. As we rocked and rolled there were howls of protest from the blokes in the back.

When I tried, as tactfully as I could, to remonstrate and suggested we went slower, looked for a 'trig' point, whatever that was, or tried to find a map reference, my boss got really wild, 'You're always talking about getting guidance. Why don't you try to get some now!' he shouted at me. 'Alright, if only you'll shut up for a minute, I'll try!' I replied, losing *my* temper. A short, rather cross silence followed, and then I prayed for direction.

I looked up at the horizon. Still nothing. The suddenly something caught my eye — there was a twinkle! The sun catching an empty petrol can may be, far away in the distance, over on the right. 'Aim for that twinkle', I said.

He swung the truck hard over to a great roar of protest from the back. We reached the top of the unsuspected, slight undulation and from there, on the skyline, we could see a line of makeshift telegraph poles with a wire on them. Civilisation! Sure enough, the wire led us to a signals camp. They lent us a tent for the night and gave us food and warm hospitality and in the morning told us the way.

Last thing that night, after I'd said my very grateful prayers and we were all tucked up, my OC came in and said to us all, 'You know, we were lost today, but it's thanks to his praying that we're here!' It's because of incidents like these that I believe anyone sincerely trying to be obedient to the will of God can receive direction, in big things and in the everyday things. The mind boggles at the immediate change which could start to take place in the world with even a relatively few people totally committed to living that way.

Of course, there was an atmosphere during the war, especially noticeable up in the desert, perhaps a greater realisation of need, which helped to make men's minds more receptive to a possible spiritual answer to problems, but how close to catastrophe do we have to get before we stop and listen and change?

A month or so later, after my experience with the maintenance corps, we found ourselves near the detachment where the sergeant was who had asked me to write his letters for him. I also heard he'd slipped back and was again taking it out on the men, calling unnecessary parades and inspections which were upsetting everyone concerned and, incidentally, not helping himself either! The challenge now was, do I look him up and perhaps get chewed up, or let him stew in it?

This was the after lunch siesta time, the hot part of the day, and *very* hot, too. He probably wouldn't relish being disturbed. I also wanted to rest, and I didn't want to have the bad news of his defection confirmed. However, I had a strong feeling to go. So off I set, walking. After a little while I found the camp, with all its bivvy tents and vehicles spread well out over quite a big area, as a precaution against any surprise air attack. After waking up one or two wrong tents, I finally found the sergeant's HQ living room ambulance. Taking my courage in both hands, and in great trepidation, I knocked on the door.

Sure enough, although he seemed friendly enough, he informed me the experience hadn't lasted. The sense of newness and starting afresh had faded, and, above all, his wife hadn't written to him for six weeks. He was afraid she'd gone off with another man, and altogether life was rotten!

We strolled out into the desert for a short distance, talked things through, then sat down on some rocks, with the sun blazing down, and he re-dedicated his life to God and decided he would trust Him to look after his wife for him. We prayed together, and then I left.

I think it was the next day that all six weeks' supply of letters arrived together for him from his wife. How they got delayed is just one of those things, but the miracle for him was getting the renewed faith in God, in his wife and in God's care for her welfare, *before* he got his mail!

There were many times like this, unexpected meetings and touches: getting to know a fellow, perhaps he would make a decision to put his trust in God and let Him run his life, then his unit would move away. You'd go off to one country, Israel perhaps, and he to another, Libya maybe, but your paths would cross again months later, and he and you, too, could renew your decisions and determination together.

5

Back to Tobruk, in a Hurry!

Now back to our journey. Cyrenaica was so beautiful, reminiscent of parts of Surrey — Camberly Heath, Chobham Common and the district where we did our army training. On and on. I began to think we would never stop. Perhaps we were heading for Benghazi? Giovanni Berta was one brief stop and then, at last, we arrived at an evacuated farmhouse at Mameli, I believe it was called.

Here we settled in gratefully. This was it! No more driving for a bit. We actually had a roof over our heads, trees around, an Arab village nearby which I never did get to see, and a few Arabs calling occasionally to trade the odd chicken for army tea or some such commodity. Our cook's ruse to dry off our used tea leaves and use them as barter was soon rumbled.

With the prospect of regular fresh meat coming along and the use of the farm kitchen, although fairly primitive, I volunteered to cook for my OC and myself. Not that I knew much about cooking, mind you, but I felt I couldn't help but improve on the sort of army cooking we'd been getting.

Hardly had we settled in, barely unpacked in fact, when an urgent message came through. We were to withdraw at once. Not retreat, of course, but withdraw. A very subtle difference!

We were so reluctant to leave 'our' lovely little farmhouse that we treated the orders with a rather self-conscious display of British phlegm and stiff upper-lips, and no sense of urgency whatever. We dallied over breakfast and dawdled over the loading-up before we finally said farewell to the farm, and set off to rejoin the coast road we'd so recently and triumphantly advanced on.

It was only then that we realised the magnitude and seriousness of this 'strategic withdrawal'. The road was solid with retreating men, vehicles, guns, tanks, the lot. Napoleon wasn't in it when it came to retreating! His men leaving Moscow may have had snow and ice to contend with, but we had heat and sand and dust, and an enemy hot on our heels!

It began to dawn on me that, apart from the crawling pace and traffic jams, we were not going to be able to stop off until we got to Tobruk. Remembering the long haul up, it was a pretty daunting prospect. All that day we pushed on, secretly regretting our leisurely getaway.

As night fell, another nightmarish phenomenon developed: if you were driving, you couldn't keep your eyes open, but as soon as you were relieved, you woke up! Wetting your eyelids with spit, holding your head out of the window to get what sultry air there was on your face — nothing seemed to work. We daren't pull off the road surface onto the deep, loose, sandy verges, for we might never get back on again! The only thing that kept us going was the thought that, eventually, we would be able to lie down and go to sleep.

The fight against falling asleep while driving, with all the repercussions of falling into the ditch, possible injury, the hold-up of the men and traffic who were in the massive retreat behind us, is the strongest memory of that awful crawl back, with its sense of victory in the immediate future quite dashed. Added to this was the knowledge that even if it was only for the time, maybe, and if the army were able to hold out against the enemy at some point, Tobruk perhaps, we would still have to come all this way back, and that without the excitement and stimulation of the novelty and discovery of new territory.

I suppose we must have reported in at Tobruk and had some food in the early hours of the next morning, in the blackout, but my memory is decidedly hazy about all that. Eventually we found ourselves camping in a declivity or fold of the land running parallel to the road leading into the town. There were anemones blooming everywhere, Spring in the desert, I guess. It was good not to be on the move. Peace at last! Not for long, though. The 'peace' was soon rudely shattered by very low flying Stukas swooping over the ridge and machine-gunning us periodically. We didn't stay there very long!

Quite soon, we got the order to split the unit up. Some to carry on to the new defence line nearer to Egypt, and some to stay behind as part of the new garrison to hold Tobruk, while the 'tide of war' swept round and past us. That was the hope, anyway! The rather ominous suggestion came next, that the unmarried men should 'volunteer' to stay. As my OC was in charge, although he was married, and I was unmarried, and incidentally his driver, we were natural 'volunteers'.

To make the situation seem even more threatening, we were ordered to pack up all our bits and pieces, my Clydella pyjamas, the big Moffatt translation of the Old and New Testaments, my snapshot album, various souvenirs, in fact anything over and above the Army minimum, to be taken off to the comparative safety of the new base, and, we wondered, eventually to our next of kin?

We felt rather heroic becoming part of the second and, we were quite sure, equally successful and historic garrison of Tobruk as the Australian garrison had been. We were following in the footsteps of the incredible Aussies who had held on and served as a tangible proof that we would be ultimately victorious in the Desert, and eventually in Europe and the Pacific.

Our new camp was just outside the town, within the perimeter of barbed wire and minefields. We were on top of an escarpment, on one side of a wadi. Down below we could see a South African camp, which formed the garrison this time.

One unhappy episode happened while we were there. At dead of night we had an emergency call to take the ambulances out through the wire and into the minefield, led by men on foot who knew the very narrow, winding 'safe' track, to pick up some British wounded who had been captured by the Germans, but who had escaped by collaring some enemy trucks and getting back to the heavily manned perimeter.

In the dark, with German markings on the vehicles, our patrol, understandably perhaps, suspected a trick and opened fire on them, with devastating effect. It was a grisly, ghastly end to what must have been a pretty harrowing experience: to reach safety and then be shot up by your own side.

Life settled down once more to a routine. Fairly regular bombardments, the regular, irregular attacks on the perimeter and the moving of casualties into Tobruk hospital. We were reasonably close to the sparkling, amazingly sapphire-blue sea and the silver sandy beaches, and as the weather warmed up we had a few excursions to the seashore for swimming and sun-bathing.

Then things began to happen! Up until this time, our Red Crosses on the ambulances had given us a degree of immunity from direct attack, and we had been, as it were, spectators from a safe sideline, apart from our occasional forays into quite real danger and action. Then suddenly we began to notice strange goings-on in the wadi camp below. A certain amount of packing up was taking place and then, one evening, the fireworks started! They were blowing up their ammunition. Guns and vehicles, too, I seem to remember. All went up in smoke.

We'd heard nothing of an enemy breakthrough, or even of a threatened, massive assault, so this very impressive display of fire, smoke and explosions was spoilt somewhat by our thinking, perhaps mistakenly, that someone, somewhere, was suffering from undue pessimism, if not actual defeatism. Eventually, everything down in the wadi smouldered into an uneasy stillness, and we settled down for the night, the silence broken only by the odd bullet or shell blowing up.

The next morning, I climbed down our side of the wadi to see if I could find out what was happening. When I got to the camp, I found it completely deserted. If not exactly silently, the South Africans had, if not actually folded most of their tents, certainly stolen away!

The camp was a shambles of hurriedly abandoned kit and personal belongings, cameras, typewriters, a Rolls razor, sheets of postage stamps and bedding: all in the hectic, untidy disarray of a last minute getaway. My inbuilt instinct to retrieve and salvage surged up, and I began to collect cameras, a portable typewriter, and so on.

Then I saw it: a safari bed! Now, I'd always thought that these safari beds, so light and collapsible, yet lifting you just that much off the ground, were the height of luxury and, even without my Li-lo air mattress, could make desert life almost desirable, so I grabbed it and without stopping to dismantle it and fold it up I started to walk back along the track to where I had to climb up to our camp.

Suddenly round a bend in the track came an armoured truck with German army markings, with two young Germans and a dirty great gun mounted on it, haring along towards the abandoned camp! A blur of thoughts — was this it? Was this where the war suddenly became real for me? Was I going to be shot up or shot down out of hand, picked up or what? Feeling rather self-conscious and foolish standing there, with my cot and what have you under one arm, all I could think of to do was to give a rather half-hearted wave with my free hand. The Germans and their truck raced past with only a cursory glance in my direction.

Still clutching my precious bed and the other treasure trove, I scaled the steep side of that wadi in about five minutes flat, only to find when I reached the top that I'd shot up the wrong side and so, in all the heat of midday, I had to climb all the way down, cross the track and wearily climb up the other side to our camp. There I reported the presence of the enemy down below.

We quickly made a cache of our rifles and buried our official documents, then sat back and waited for orders. I suppose we felt that we, as an ambulance unit, should stay available for the wounded, but no orders came. Some went after more loot, and then we all had lunch.

We'd just got to the tinned peaches and evaporated milk stage, when a grim-faced young German in an open truck drove up with a pistol in his hand and said, just like the films, 'For you the war is over!' I quickly whispered to my OC, who spoke German: 'Ask him if we can finish lunch!' He did so, and our captor replied, 'Very well, but be quick, I have much to do!' Then he detailed us to take our, by now surrendered I suppose, ambulances into Tobruk hospital.

6

On My Own

I don't quite remember what our sleeping arrangements were that first night. Our ambulances and trucks were clustered together like a little lost flock of sheep in the centre of the hospital square. I can remember hiding the cameras and the typewriter in the loft beams of an empty outhouse. This was probably where I spent the night. Certainly, I well remember the next morning. True to training and habit I decided to have my early time of guidance. I went outside and sat down against the wall, hoping to be uninterrupted.

The first thought I wrote down was: 'It's no good having a quiet time, and asking God what He wants me to do — from now on the Germans are giving the orders!' (This I think was the old Devil's trick of playing on one's laziness, and sometimes even resentment of the imperative discipline of regular, early morning quiet times.) My next thought was to try listening to God. Sure enough a thought came, which I wrote down: 'Don't sit around waiting for the Germans to tell you what to do. Go and do something useful in one of the wards.'

I had a quick prayer and went off to the hospital. The ward I picked on looked like Hampstead Heath after a Bank holiday. Why it should have got so untidy and the floor littered so badly, so quickly, I don't know. Perhaps the orderlies had beaten it to Egypt before the enemy arrived.

Anyhow, the patients were desperate for bottles, to wash, to eat, and for news. After the first emergency crack round, I began to sweep the ward. I suppose there were others there working with me, but for the life of me, all I can remember after sweeping through was thinking it must be time for breakfast, and so out I went. I looked at my watch and to my amazement it was eleven o'clock. All my mates had disappeared. They had been marched off to the 'cage' to join the 25,000 other prisoners taken in the fall of Tobruk shambles.

So I stayed. No one knew I was there. I was independent and, so to speak, my own boss. I thought it would be interesting to work in the operating theatre, so off I went and attached myself to the valiant band of massively overworked surgeons carrying on, in spite of smashed windows, flies, no sterilised or hygienic atmosphere, and not much of anything else. They carried on with amputations, the removal of shell fragments, the stitching up of nearly torn-off muscles, and all the patching up that follows in the aftermath of a fierce rearguard action.

My first job was in the lobby of the operating theatre for about twenty or thirty stretcher cases, all by now just lying on the ground, wounded and suffering from shock. The shock had rendered them incapable of relieving themselves, and all were suffering extreme discomfort with distended stomachs. Although I'd never seen such an instrument before, after one demonstration with a catheter I was able to manage, and soon they were all much more comfortable.

In the theatre, after two or three hasty exits to recover from near fainting and sickness at the sight of flesh being cut and the flow of blood caused by scalpels and saws in action on human bodies, I soon got used to watching operations, became a little more objective, and quite adept at swatting flies on the surgeon's bare back. These flies looked very much like our houseflies, but they possessed a sting like a cigarette burn, and of course they were a much greater distraction to the operator than the slap of the fly swatter. Holding limbs steady for amputation was another job, and I was amazed to see the crudity of some of these operations.

The surgeon with whom I worked was very understanding and efficient, and used to explain what he was doing as he went along, just as if we were medical students at a teaching hospital. We worked, it seemed, the clock round.

After a few days there was a dramatic interruption. Suddenly the door of the theatre burst open and in stalked a little band of Germans: doctors, surgeons and their bodyguard. One fellow in particular caught my eye, a dapper, dynamic little man. He was a typical Nazi in jackboots and riding breeches, the Afrika Korps desert cap, of course, and a gun in his hand. They proved to be the takeover team.

They seemed not to know about drip treatment for shock, or to be much used to anaesthetics either, come to that, and were immediately keenly interested in these aspects of British surgery. Whether they thought we were advanced in technique or just soft, I never found out.

After the switch, they brought in some very tough-looking nursing sisters. They looked more like charladies. I may be doing them an injustice, perhaps their clothing was their army's idea of being practical. They weren't above doing any stretcher bearing needed. It was a surprise, too, to find women so close to the firing line.

I was able to continue looking after the British wounded, and as the officer types regained some measure of health, they were flown out, to Germany I imagined. One of the jobs I took on with a South African padre was kitting them out, as far as we could, with clothes for the journey. Dead men's clothes mostly, I suspect. By one of those amazing 'coincidences', this padre turned out to be the very first C of E clergyman I had met in the Oxford Group way back in 1936, though only once briefly in his parish of Penge, in England, before he retired to South Africa. Of course, we had many mutual friends.

About this time, the British CSM at the hospital was ordered by the Germans, who were now in charge, to make a roll-call of all the British staff in the hospital, and he decided to put me on it. I felt at the time very resentful at what I felt was a betrayal of my unofficial presence there. I thought it was a dirty trick. It meant that from then on I had to go on parades and, of course, I'd lost my free option of what to do and which jobs to take on.

However, Colonel Davey, officer-in-charge at the hospital until the takeover, made it one of his last jobs to issue us all with 'Protected Personnel', Geneva Convention, Red Cross Cards. This was to have remarkable consequences, of which more later.

One afternoon, after a heavy stretch of work in the morning, I decided to have a siesta on my 'stretcher' bed, when I heard my name being shouted out in the square. Being deaf in one ear, I'd not heard the original order for an extra parade and so I decided to ignore the shouts. I felt I'd done enough for one day. Eventually I was found and hauled before the German CSM and sternly reprimanded. This was the first of my two encounters with him.

The second was after a spectacular air raid on Tobruk harbour by British planes. The hospital, being on top of a hill, was like a grandstand and as the planes swept in to drop their bombs, they seemed to be almost eye-level. Some bombs dropped on the town, some uncomfortably close, but it was an awe-inspiring and encouraging sight to see our air force hitting back at last. It was a great morale booster.

The next morning there were two unexploded bombs lying in the hospital precincts. There were photographers taking pictures of them from all angles, carefully including Red Crosses on the buildings in the backgrounds. You can imagine the propaganda that was going to made out of them: 'British bomb hospital!' Well, unexploded they may have been, but to me they looked like deliberate plants. There weren't even any dents in the ground.

The second of these bombs was right in the middle of the hospital square. It was lunch-time, but everyone had taken cover, except for the two poor Africans who had the job of lifting the bomb on to a hand cart and shifting it out to the desert, where it could be detonated harmlessly.

I had two thoughts: one, to show my disbelief that the RAF would bomb hospitals by going across casually to inspect the 'bomb', and two, to short cut across the square and so get myself in the front of the lunch queue. Everyone was cowering under cover and peeping round walls and blast barriers! I got as far as the bomb, when the German CSM stood out from his cover and shouted: 'Halt! What do you think you are doing?' I replied that I was on my way to lunch and, anyway, it wasn't a real bomb, was it?

He was very cross and when I began to continue on my way towards lunch, he picked up a stone and threw it at me to emphasise his command to 'Halt!' He missed, but he kept me there until the operation was completed. I don't know whether I proved my point, but afterwards he told me I was a trouble-maker and I'd have to go!

That afternoon, he took me personally in his little army two-seater, up to the 'cage'. On our way out of the town, he stopped on the brow of the hill and we looked back at a panoramic view of the port. Against the brilliant blue sky, there was a vast, inverted cone of black, billowing smoke, belching up from the successfully bombed oil dump. My heart sang, but I didn't dare even smile. He said nothing but, oh, how his expression showed his feelings.

7

'Caged'

At the 'cage', a heavily barbed-wired compound, with a few tents for kitchen and administration, all of which had been hastily thrown together a month previously to help cope with the sudden mass of prisoners, I found all the inmates were African or Indians. This was strange and foreign to me, to say the least.

Added to this unexpected environment, dumped there without the company of any of my former mates, I found to my horror that when I accidentally brushed up against one of the black tents, they weren't black at all, but simply black with masses of flies! You could hear the angry buzz as they took off, when disturbed, like a swarm of bees. The dug-outs were the same. Flies everywhere. Perhaps it was because the camp was on the site of the British Army NAAFI, with the subsequent pollution, but the situation was nightmarish.

Fortunately, a little Indian sergeant was unexpectedly forthcoming and very friendly. He welcomed me, showed me the 'amenities', and explained the order of things, or, rather, the haphazard lack of order. He did much to help me settle in. It wasn't until sometime later that I discovered that the copious notes he kept making in his notebook were not of my profound wit and wisdom, but of any new words of English! He was determined to learn the language properly, and so jotted down notes and added to his vocabulary all the time.

That evening, some battle-scarred, war-weary New Zealanders, 'Kiwis', were hustled in with us, and I attached myself to them. They very generously let me share the few bivouac tents and rations they still had.

It must have been the next day the Kiwis and I were put in trucks and driven off in convoy along the long, long road on which we had so recently retreated. We spent the first night in a hastily constructed 'cage', in what some said was an Arab cemetery.

The following day, bowling along in our crowded trucks, the convoy was reduced to a crawl at one point. Parked on the side of the road were German and Italian cars and trucks, and standing to watch us pass, the unmistakeable figure of Mussolini himself. As he stood there, an aide came up to him with a shot gun, which he cocked casually over one arm. Perhaps he was afraid that some prisoner or other might go berserk and attack him, to try and release some of the quite literally, pent-up feelings we all had.

Some long way along the road, we came to a semi-permanent camp, a sudden deep, declivity in the other wise flat desert, which we called 'The Palm Tree Oasis', after the dusty trees we found there. This was near Benghazi, I believe. As we dismounted and queued to go into the enclosure, rumours began to circulate: 'Get rid of your food reserves, they'll be taken from you, and cameras, knives, etc.'

They certainly took my last remaining 'looted' camera from me. My knife I managed to hide and I kept my watch. The food which we all ate up so unnecessarily or gave away, or even threw away to keep it out of the enemy's hands, would have been safe enough. If we had known of the awful, monotonous diet of boiled, unsalted rice and dull, tasteless biscuits we were going to have to live on, it could easily have been made to last and so lend a little interest. I remember I had a big tin of Marmite, but as at that stage our palates and appetites were still reasonably civilised and choosy, I had tired of its taste, and I gave it away. Many times later I wished I'd still got it, to flavour the rice and add the touch of saltiness to our salt-starved diet.

There seemed to be a real shortage of salt and also, perhaps more understandably, of sugar. Salt, so taken for granted, soon revealed itself as a basic necessity of living and one's body began demanding it. The excessive heat of the day and the resulting perspiration all added to the loss of salt and revealed the need.

Now began a series of what I can only call personal miracles. Before I'd left Tobruk I had begun to realise that the whole experience of being a fully-fledged prisoner-of-war, with its prospects of privation, dirt and uncertain duration was too much for me to face alone. I needed a new, deeper, constant touch with God and realisation of His Presence, and so I had got hold of a clergyman friend, and in the privacy of the hospital chapel, I opened my heart to him and shared, confessed if you like, all the compromises and defeats that had cropped up and crept into my daily living.

For instance, in spite of the moral decadence of my life earlier, because of the 'respectability' of my upbringing, I had never come across any pornographic literature, and also, the same shy 'respectability' prevented me from ever going into a shop and spending my hard-earned cash on the stuff. It wasn't until I was taken prisoner that in the course of my jobs in the hospital I came across one of these novels. Although badly written, or perhaps just badly translated, it was compulsive reading. I'd never imagined that such stuff was ever written, let alone printed!

I had made the usual excuses of myself, such as: 'It was my duty to be informed, etc.,' but the effect on my mind had been calamitous and, of course, the book had to be destroyed. After this, recurring memories had to be dealt with. First the look, then the thought, then the action, and perhaps a whole new habit of unconsciously tainted living could be under way.

This opening of the heart to another person, holding nothing back, apart from its Biblical authority, 'Confess your sins, one to another, that ye may be healed', James 5:16, is such sound common and psychological sense. It gives a very real sense of being cleansed, and the slate being washed clean. It makes real the conviction of God's forgiveness, and His continuing presence and care for you. Every day a fresh, completely new beginning. It can be as invigorating as a cold shower and every bit as refreshing.

This rocky hollow, with its not unlimited water supply, became 'home' for us. The height of luxury became a rock you could lean against during the day, and formed a protection for your head at night. There was just enough ground in front of it to be able to dispose your body round and over the fixed small stones and rocks, and a little 'hip hole' which turned the whole, hard surface into a seeming feather bed! At times a flash of silver would make us feel a snake was dashing across us, but I rather think it must have been a fairly big lizard. The lizards never stopped long enough for us to examine them.

The mosquitoes were a real menace at night. After waking up one morning with swollen lips and lumps on my forehead, I thankfully used a small piece of green net, about eighteen inches square, which I had salvaged, as a mini-mosquito net. I'd saved it for no other reason than that it might come in useful sometime.

It was in this camp that dysentery really got hold of us. I think nearly everyone got it. The top soil on the rocks was at most only two feet deep, so the latrines were never adequate and frequently overflowed. The long boxes with eight or nine holes covering the trench for our use were always black with flies. Disease was bound to spread.

The water pressure in the oasis spring was enough to enable a couple of showers to be rigged up, but obviousiy there wasn't enough water to last all the time, so they were only turned on at midday for an hour or two. This was the hottest time of the day, everyone was flaked out. It required real moral and physical effort to get yourself across the few hundred yards of burning, hot sand and while keeping an eye on your clothes, fight your way into the mud patch and the milling throng of enthusiasts, and get yourself under, if you were lucky, the trickle of water called a shower! The only other alternative was to reach up with your hands over the men's heads and try to divert some water in your direction.

One morning, I had the thought to wash all my clothes, the khaki drill, underwear, socks and also to darn all my socks. Under these circumstances, with no work or entertainment laid on, it was always nice to spread out jobs, a bit today, something to do tomorrow and so on, so you can imagine I had a bit of a mental rebellion about this thought. However, I stuck to the discipline and obeyed. I washed everything (it dried in ten minutes, in that heat), checked and darned my socks.

The next day, to everyone's complete surprise, we were marched out of the oasis with its few palm trees, rocks and spasmodic water supply up to waiting transport and taken to the vast cages, treeless and waterless, which were serving as transit camps. One pint of water per man, per day, and brackish at that. I don't quite remember whether we had an extra ration of water, even more tainted, for washing, all I can remember is the six of us in our little group sharing a tin hat full of this water. On one occasion, I remember seeing a six-foot fellow, he may have been the last to go, actually standing, rather precariously, in the hat and trying to wash all over. The water must have been a bit soupy by that time, practically a mud pack. His intentions were hygienic, anyhow!

While we were in the oasis I had time to develop

a latent urge for sketching. I hesitate to call it a talent, although it was completely natural, a hangover from schooldays. Very strangely, I discovered I could not remember the actual constitution of flowers, botanically speaking. This was the more odd because botany and flowers had always been a strong interest. How many petals, in what order, and so on, had slipped my memory completely, so flowers were out as subjects.

When I started drawing my neighbours, I found I could catch a likeness. Very soon I was in demand. The Maoris particularly wanted their pictures drawn, or the fern emblem of the Kiwis. Somewhere in New Zealand there may be 'masterpieces' of mine still in existence. It's a nice thought.

In this 'Palm Tree Oasis', men began to make decisions and to change. Perhaps the introduction would come from someone seeing me reading my pocket copy of Moffatt's translation of the New Testament, and asking to borrow it, or just through turning the conversation away from negative moaning and groaning about life in general, and in their opinion its purposelessness, towards the whole experience of change, and of doing God's will.

There were eventually four of us, at the oasis, who used to meet every morning early. One was, I believe, a painter on Sydney Bridge, Australia. A continuous, monotonous job, if ever there was one, which, when you'd finished, you just went back to the beginning again! Another was a young Kiwi, Dave, who really got the message that God had a plan for all men, all the time. He even realised that it wasn't our job to pray for our release, or for a transfer to better conditions, but to find out and do God's will where we were, trusting Him to provide for all our needs now and in the future.

During our prayers together, which we said out loud to include each other, Dave would pray for this, but the other two nearly always asked to be moved on from this very dodgy, dysentery-plagued spot, and to be shipped speedily to somewhere in Europe, Italy perhaps. Well, they did get out on the next shipment, but this was unfortunately sunk by one of our own vessels by mistake and, although there was no loss of life, they lost all their remaining bits and pieces. It must have been a terrifying and most uncomfortable experience. We heard all about this when we arrived in Italy, later. This willingness to be where God wants you to be can mean reassurance, inner peace and a preparedness to capitalise on any situation or set of circumstances that may arise.

When we arrived at the coiled barb-wired, completely flat and featureless transit camp compounds near Benghazi, we were confronted with a vast sea of 'bivvy' tents. There were three or four of these compounds and eventually we were hived off to our own particular section.

8

Transit Camps

That first evening I had a stroll round the camp, keeping carefully to the main avenues so that I would not get lost and be unable to find my way back to my mates. Halfway along the broad avenue between the hundreds of tents, I suddenly saw a face I'd last seen in 'civvy' street, in England, just before the war. It seemed a lifetime ago! Stanley was no better than the rest of us physically, perhaps worse, but both of us swapped news and stories which lifted our hearts and spirits, almost as if we had received mail from home. We arranged to meet daily from then on, but unfortunately for that arrangement, I was moved out with the next batch into one of the neighbouring 'cages'.

All was not lost, however, although it seemed tragic to be separated from an old friend so soon. The next day, after we moved, was a Sunday and a captured padre, who was allowed to move from camp to camp to take services for us all in turn, came to us.

To my amazement, his sermon was a vague, pious generalisation, a, dare I say it, conventional address, completely unrelated to the situation we were in. There was nothing to give us faith and trust, reassurance, peace of mind or fan the flames of perhaps failing or failed faith.

I made a bee-line for him afterwards. At least he might be able to take a message to Stanley in the other compound. Something I said prompted him to tell me he'd been in touch with MRA but that back in South Africa, which was now his home, he had drifted away from it. He had become, as I'd seen and heard, ineffective and dull. Well, we talked. I told him news and, miraculously, he caught fire! He even managed to find my friend among the hundreds in the other camp. The next time he came to preach his sermon was real dynamite.

Whether it was due to increasing weakness and discomfort from the dysentery and dirt, or a sense of impermanence about this so-called transit camp, I don't know, but although chaps were still interested in borrowing my pocket 'Moffatt', and one or two came to make decisions to let God run their lives, it was very much a case of putting people in touch with God and trusting Him to look after them. All decisions were made with Him anyway, I was only the witness of the procedure. This is always so, of course, but usually one has the opportunity of continuing with fellowship and backing-up.

It was in this camp that I discovered just how much weight I'd lost. There was a medical tent in the next compound and those of us who wanted a change of routine, or clung hopefully to our faith in the medical profession, were marched through on sick parade.

In the waiting section of the marquee there were

some wooden benches, and with a sigh of relief I sat down, only to spring up as though I had been stung! I thought two nails must be sticking up on the seat. After all the seatless weeks lying down on the ground, I'd not realised how much flesh I had lost, and I found that I was virtually sitting on my 'bare' bones. This was disturbing to say the least, and I accepted two white tablets from the Italian medico, which seemed to be the limit of the treatment, with hopeful gratitude. They had no effect at all and so I didn't make the effort again.

We could see Benghazi as a black, serrated, distant silhouette on the skyline. This I tried to sketch, not very successfully. It wasn't until we reached Italy and I had the temerity to mobilise an art class, when one of my 'pupils' was able to give me a few tips on perspective and help me in the use of foreground, that I began to get a sense of far distance.

A sneaking fear at the back of my mind at this time was of having to fall out, because of my upset tummy, from the column of marching POWs during the journey on foot that lay ahead. This was to the port of Benghazi for our embarkation for Italy. I did not want to lose touch with the immediate band of companions I had got used to, and become friendly with, during our forced proximity. I prayed about this and, thankfully, I found that a temporary healing took place, and the long march to the ship was uncomplicated by my dysentery.

The march, though wearisome, was made almost enjoyable by the exciting thought of going back to Europe, either Germany or Italy, which was the accepted drill for POWs. Perhaps it was just the fear of being left behind that gave me this remission, so that I was able to keep up with the others.

On the ship, at last, we were packed like sardines, almost literally, in the hold. I don't think anyone had any free space round him. We were all touching, both sides, and if you turned over, it could start a chain reaction!

It was here, inevitably I suppose in those cramped conditions, that I collected my first louse, the first of many. Whether I got it from my too-close companions, or the palliasses we were on, I don't know, but there to my horror, it was! These creatures with their pin-sized, crablike heads, and fat little tails which stuck up in the air in a kind of ecstasy as they bit into you and proceeded to fill themselves up with your blood, became one of the biggest sources of irritation, in every sense of the word, during our prison life. From then on we had the lice as well as dysentery and near-starvation to contend with.

The prospect of sea-sickness and the non-existence of washing facilities, plus the very real possibility of accidental attacks on the ship by our own submarines or whatever, all added to a great feeling of vulnerability. It brought too, an overwhelming sense of need, a strong need of faith in God, and a continuing belief that God cared and was caring for me.

A remarkable demonstration of this care came over sugar, or rather the lack of it. Our rations on board ship were 4-inch square biscuits, unsalted, unsweetened and quite tasteless, as our literally 'hard' rations, and water. The biscuits were so hard you could hardly break them. There was only one thing to do to make them eatable, dip bits in the water. This was an awful diet for me, with my carefully cultivated, probably over-indulged, sweet tooth, and as time passed in these awful conditions of overcrowding, I found myself getting more and more irritable with my immediate neighbours, in fact I began to feel I hated all mankind!

Suddenly, I got the conviction that it was the lack of sweetness and saltiness in what passed as food that was making me feel so depressed, cross and short-tempered. I asked for the answer and got it — just like that! 'Give up wanting and demanding sugar. Be willing, and tell God you're willing, never to have sugar again'. This I did, in spite of my fears that He might take me up on it. Immediately the tension went and, although the biscuits still only tasted of flour and water, I didn't seem to mind any more.

Now, here is the amazing thing. Almost within minutes I had to make a dash for the deck, up the ladder to the makeshift latrines. On my way back, I passed three or four German soldiers, who were going home on convalescent leave or something, having their breakfast on deck. As I went by, one of them handed me a couple of white grapes — and were they sweet? They seemed like solid sugar! Was this God's answer to my willingness? His reassurance that all was not lost?

It became the custom of some of the Germans, after their meals, to toss the few spare rolls of bread down to us through the open hatch. An extraordinary happening would then take place: it seemed as if, from a completely prone position on the floor of the hold, all the men in that area rose like a cloud of starlings, with hands outstretched, reaching for these precious few rolls! How they managed to levitate themselves, I don't know, but a most undignified, free-for-all scramble took place, much to the amusement of the Germans above. Being quite impossibly distant from the area where the rolls were being dropped, I allowed myself to feel shocked and horrified at the undisciplined carry-on — 'letting the British down!' and all that. I wonder what I would have done, had I been nearer? Been killed in the rush, I expect, probably with a bread roll clutched in my despairing hand!

9

Italy

After sounds of distant gunfire in the night and the usual rumours that we were being attacked by a British submarine, we eventually arrived at Bari, in the tip of Italy. Curiously, the sounds of gunfire in the distance, even with the fear of possible sinking, were reassuring in a strange sort of way. As in the air raid in Tobruk, they signified the presence of our friends and allies, on the offensive. In any case, I was quite sure, irrationally, of course, that *our* bombs and shells wouldn't hurt *us*! You also felt, paradoxically, that even the awful conditions you were in, were at least preferable to milling about in the sea, hoping to be picked up.

In Bari, we were disembarked, marshalled into some sort of order and marched off through the town, under the apathetic gaze of the early workers, in the misty, rather chilly, dawn.

There seemed to be a detour through an olive grove to a camp of bell tents. Here we settled in for a week or two. We were formed up into groups of, I think, seven to a tent, showered and had our hair cropped, whether for hygiene or to make us more easily identifiable in case of any attempted escape, I don't know.

It was here that we received our first Red Cross parcels. This was a tremendous event. We'd heard of them from the same source which in any group of soldiers seems to have all the inside 'griff', or information. The prospect of these parcels had done much to keep up our morale and sustain our spirits, but with their arrival we had unexpected problems. These parcels were meant for individuals, but at this stage we only had one parcel per tent of seven men! Our NCO types did their valiant best, and as each tin was opened it was meticulously spooned out into seven 'equal' portions — but what to use for containers to keep things apart? Meat and veg, from the sweet things, margarine from bacon, the condensed milk from the tea and cocoa, even jam. Tin lids, bits of paper, anything possible, was pressed into service to keep them separated, and to try and make these few mouthfuls last as long as possible.

At this stage, I still had my childhood dislike of cheese and prunes and, believe it or not, I used to give them away! However, during our journeys I had formed a sporadic sort of friendship with a sergeant, going by the nickname of 'Griff', for the obvious reason that he was always seemingly able to be one jump ahead of anyone with any news or information.

He was an extraordinary fellow, a Yorkshireman, and our friendship was a kind of guerilla warfare. He was very irascible and sometimes, in spite of great care on my part, I would occasionally react and there would be a flaming row, followed always by an apology on my part for my lack of patience or whatever. After all, one is always a bit to blame in any row. He was very helpful on many occasions. He was in the RAMC I think.

'Griff' looked after me like a father. He tried to stop me saving a slice of my raw, issued onion and a bite of the tiny bread roll overnight, for a kind of breakfast. He told me the onion would go off once it was cut, become poisonous in fact. However, as I couldn't face the prospect of waiting until 11 am the next day for the next issue of rations: a tiny bread roll, a medium-sized raw onion, and then later a mouthful of cheese, to last us until the evening watery, vegetable soup, all or any of which might not arrive on time, or at all, I persisted. This was one bone of contention.

He didn't think it was healthy for me to get up so early and sit out in the cold dawn for my quiet time. These were the sort of things we rowed about, but he did have a profound influence, physically, on my life at this time and, even more importantly, at a later stage, in our final concentration camp, PG 70. He *begged* me to try eating cheese and prunes. He suggested I put the cheese on my bread with marmalade, in the Yorkshire manner. With my involuntarily purified taste, I found it was superb, out of this world! The prunes, either dry or, if you could force yourself to wait, soaked in water, were more like sugar-candy than fruits. To this day, I eat and enjoy all kinds of cheeses, even the high-smelling ones, though only once or twice with jam or marmalade.

While we were in this camp, I cut up and made my soft wool British army blanket, which I'd carefully kept with me, into a ground-length 'dressing gown'. I added buttons, which I'd nicked off the Italian tent, so that I could turn it up during the day and wear it as an overcoat. A spare piece made a hood to button on at night. The days were getting cooler, and the nights were quite cold by now. The thread I was able to unpick from the blanket ends. The buttons on the tents were probably part of their packing-up and transporting system, I suppose.

When we came to move out of this place to go to our final (we hoped) camp, the Italians tried to confiscate my dressing-gown cum overcoat, wool being at a premium in Italy. However, I stood my ground more courageously than usual, and insisted it was British Army issue, and it *was* mine. Perhaps because of my dutch courage determination not to surrender my sartorial masterpiece, but more likely because of the pressure of the queue behind me, they let me through and I kept it. Very useful it proved too, although I must admit it didn't start a fashion!

At the railway station in Bari we were herded into cattle trucks, the traditional form of transport for prisoners-of-war. One could only hope the journey would be short. There were no seats and only by the occasional great effort could one pull oneself up to the little slit windows at the top of the truck's sides and catch a glimpse of the countryside through which our train crawled and climbed.

Interestingly, this southern tip of Italy resembled very closely the type of landscape we had just left in Benghazi. Even the peasant women seemed to be the same, dressed in black, barefoot and carrying their belongings bundled up and balanced precariously on their heads.

I don't know the route we took, or whether we

diverted from the direct route, but I swear I caught a glimpse of a railway station in Rome, of all places, and had a first, quick look at 'city' civilians on the platform. The women looked very smart. There was no great interest shown in our cattle trucks, and the pause was only short. Perhaps they wanted to disclaim or ignore the fact that there were men inside, travelling like animals. An apathetic attitude which had more sinister implications in some other countries!

An amusing thing happened on the journey, which could not have happened in the British Army. We halted at a big railway junction. Across the maze of lines there was a large wine-making factory, or should it be distillery? With one accord, our guards, who seemed to know it, left the train and us, nipped across the railway tracks, and before we knew what was happening, were coming back with bunches of grapes in their arms, eating as they came.

One guard was stopped by a wildly gesticulating officer. Obviously the guard's explanation did not please the officer, who promptly slapped the man across the face, both sides, with his gloves in the approved 'duelling' manner! This caused the chap, in his surprise, to drop his grapes. Rashly, he bent down to pick them up. This was too much for the officer: he let fly at the inviting backside, and the guard landed on his face! This was hilarious farce and those of us who could see out, roared with laughter. A simple incident, but so well timed, so human and so unmilitary.

There were no real toilet facilities in our truck and as my dysentery had returned, I suffered great discomfort. Even if the train stopped on the track I was not allowed off, for fear I might try to escape I suppose. The dilemma was solved eventually by our two guards, each holding one of my hands, holding me out over the side, through the open door. The relief, though temporary, was great enough to offset any embarrassment I might have felt, and the sense of the ridiculousness of the situation did not occur to me until later. In fact, it was probably the two guards who were embarrassed!

At last, our collection of cattle trucks chuffed jerkily but thankfully to a halt, after a most uncomfortable stop/start journey up into the hills, at a small village station called Monturano.

On the other side of an ill-defined road or square was the entrance to a big concrete factory complex, with a big signboard across: 'Campo Concentramento PG 70'. Was this to be 'home'? It was!

10

Campo Concentramento PG 70

We were marshalled into some sort of order, and began shuffling our way through the gates, past a crowd of prisoners who had been there some time, pressed up against the fence, eagerly looking for friends or to hear the latest news of the war. All of our news was, of course, months' old and they soon cleared off while we went to be issued with palliasses, straw to put in them, and blankets. The bunk beds for our contingent had either not arrived or had not been assembled, but the vast, empty, newly-built canning factory buildings were there and so we bedded down on the concrete floor.

One of the first things I did was to get into trouble. Inside the compound there was a foot high trip wire, running all round the camp, about ten or twelve feet from the high wire fence. Later, I found out the idea was for prisoners not to cross this wire to approach the fence. In its protected state the grass had grown lush and full of wild flowers. To my deprived artistic/botanic senses this was beautiful and I instinctively stepped across to pick one of the flowers to sketch.

Immediately there was pandemonium! From the look-out tower the guard trained his gun on me, there were shouts from every direction, and it was indicated forcefully and hysterically that I should halt and stand. From the guard-house a motley crew of odd-sized, heavily armed men came running at the double and surrounded me. Anxiously, I couldn't help wondering whether this was where all the terrors, solitary confinements and interrogations were going to come true for me.

At the double, I was rapidly shuttled off to the guard-room which was full of British NCOs, with Italians telling them of procedures, roll calls, food issues and so on.

I was trying to explain my artistic appreciation of the Italian wild flowers and my urge to draw them, when one of the British types remembered my efforts at the 'Oasis' camp and explained that I did actually draw flowers, and, incidentally, drew people as well.

The Italian Camp Commandant, a short, stocky, dark, curly-haired man, who happened to be in the office, intervened at this point and said to me, 'OK, draw me!' He then proceeded to sit on the table and posed for me!

I had no time to have any qualms about my ability, but he seemed to like the result alright. While capturing a likeness, my sketches always seemed to heighten the sitter's better features and he turned out looking very impressive, rather like one of the nobler Roman emperors. He thereupon asked me to make sketches of the camp for him and sent in paper and crayons to use. I had hoped for water colours, but I was thankful for anything. My trespassing was understood and overlooked, and I was a 'relatively' free man again.

The commandant became a kind of friend and whenever we met when he was on his rounds, he would greet me. As he had heard about my dysentery, he always prefaced any remarks with, 'Buon Giorno, how is your stomach?' This was about the limit of his English, and as I had no Italian, we both had to make do with our schoolboy French; so my early struggles at school paid off and we did manage to widen the scope of our chats a little. (A very little!) He was a solicitor in peacetime and he proved a very kindly commandant.

Very soon our bunks were put together, built in groups of six with three semi-detached layers: two bunks almost on the floor, two in the middle and two at the top, which, surprisingly, no one seemed to want. I saw the possibilities of these 'penthouse' bunks and to my delight and relief, I was able to claim one of the top two of our six bunks.

My partner on this top deck was a Scot from Glasgow, with a broad accent. He had been unemployed ever since leaving school and conscription had been his first job ever. He was a quiet fellow, pleasant enough, and we got on alright, in a passive sort of way.

On the ground floor was a slightly older fellow who had worked for a London borough, as a road-sweeper. We were certainly a cross-section of society. This last fellow never seemed to want to leave the bunk area. Mistrust of his neighbours or a fear of missing something perhaps. He very quickly became, automatically, our 'official' receiver and quite naturally the dispenser of our cheese ration every afternoon. This he would cut up on his blanket, very carefully, into as nearly as possible, six equally-sized pieces, and each day in strict rotation, a different man would have first pick of these approximately two by one inch cubes. The next day he would have second choice and so on, through the six of us. Fair enough, but woe betide you if you were late for the dispensation: you lost your turn to pick. Believe me, not a crumb was wasted!

This ceremony was the highlight of the day, a social event, but which, however, was fraught with anxiety: would our mate's cutting hand tremble in the right direction, when it was your turn to choose first, and so on. These small lumps of cheese would be laid out on his blanket, then we all became solemn Solomons sitting in judgment and weighing mentally the merits of each irregularly shaped lump. Survival was everything!

After a few months of the roadman's handling of the cheese ration, he was discovered to have scurvy on his seldom-washed hands and with quite a few others was put into quarantine. Miraculously, none of us caught it from him.

Extra bread rolls were issued to the men who got the odd jobs such as sweeping up the camp, and there was great competition for the work. Soon we discovered that the same fellows were staying in the jobs, and although I believe a tentative attempt was made to draw up a rota, it didn't really work out. Much as I would have liked the extra bread, I decided to keep my freedom and didn't apply, preferring to be available each day to do what God might direct.

Amazingly, miraculously, and to my incredulous wonder, a plan *was* produced every day. Some reading, a little sketching, perhaps calling on a fellow across the other side of the camp who had shown some interest in the idea of learning the discipline of God's direction for his life. Sometimes it would be a visit to the Methodist padre, or the C of E man. There was an RC chaplain to make friends with and, although there was no Rabbi, there was an Orthodox Jew from a famous theatrical and literary family.

There were ten thousand of us in the camp, six hundred and fifty in each large building. It was like a small town, but all men. There was every opportunity, within the limits of the prison rules, to let go all the restrictions of normal society, slack off, and indulge in all the things one had not the time or the bad manners to do in 'civvy' street. One could wallow in despair, not wash, read all the time. I'd always wanted to grow a beard — now was the chance. I decided, however, to keep up the discipline of shaving, although there was every excuse for not doing so: cold water, little or no soap until the parcels started coming and, of course, always the possibility that my one or two surviving razor blades would eventually pack up.

When the weather grew warmer, a kind of nudism began to appear. It was a relief to get out of lice-infested clothes, for one thing. It seemed desirable to strip off, but I didn't have any thoughts to do so, so I kept my counsel and a decent amount of clothes on, waging war on the lice as best I could. It was quite commonplace to see a couple of chaps, chatting away, sitting in the sun, casually take off their shirt or shorts and sit there running their thumb nails along the seams, popping lice, all as natural and unembarrassed as you like!

Every so often, a portable shower unit with warmish water would arrive and after queueing for a while those of us who made the effort, handed over all our clothing and blankets to be, hopefully, deloused and sterilised, while we wallowed under the showers. Back, afterwards, to the bunk to make up the bed, only to find, a half hour later, that one of the chaps on a lower bunk and piled all his blankets, undeloused, on your bed, while he shook up his straw palliasse! Trying to keep clean was a rear-guard action, alright.

The camp consisted of the buildings where we slept and lived, the cook-house, the offices and a big, bare, completely empty building wherein we could entertain ourselves. This had a stage at one end.

Outside we had a parade ground, and beyond that a rough, open space, which soon began to be trampled smooth and hard, where we had our innumerable little fires for brewing up. Beyond that was an orchard of the inevitable olive trees, each tree with a grape vine trained up it. They must have been compatible, but it surprised me to see them growing so closely together. Down through the middle of all this ran an open ditch from our latrines to join a stream, beyond the wire, which ran through the bottom of the valley.

We were not supposed to use the orchard area, but surrounding it was a wide path filled with a never-ending stream of men exercising and talking. As you walked round, the one subject under discussion seemed to be food! Every man had a cookery tip or a recipe up his sleeve. Those few who hadn't were eager to learn how to cook this, or how to cook that. How to make sweets: toffee, fudge, marzipan dates and so on.

They were so serious in their interest in the subject, one began to imagine hordes of chefs being eventually let loose all over Britain! The one topic we all ought to have tried to forget was food, and yet here we all were, tantalising ourselves with these fascinating, but oh, so frustrating, thoughts.

I think it was hunger that prompted a number of us to start trying to learn Italian, so as to be able to ask for bread or an egg: 'pani', 'ova' or whatever. When we found the food was not forthcoming, I'm afraid the classes became sadly depleted.

There were comic touches in camp as well. The guards were obviously not the first class, front line, fighting types and the result when the bugle blew (a very jolly, jiglike tune) to call them on parade, was rather like a village amateur operatic chorus, all shapes and sizes, short and fat, tall and thin, all out of step and falling over one another as they ran at the double to get in line. It was hilarious!

11

Camp Industry

On one side of the camp, there was a very steep, almost a sugar loaf, hill with a small town clustered round the impressive and very beautiful cathedral. This was Fermo. With its vineyards and olive trees growing up the sides of the hill, it quickly became a favourite subject with our artists. Further away, at the bottom end of the camp, we could see in the distance another village perched on top of another very steep hill with a very lovely campanile tower.

Right down in the valley below, there must have been a road because every so often we would see a car driving along. At least we could see that there was *some* normal living going on! On the other side of the camp we could catch an occasional glimpse of very distant, snow-capped peaks. This was where Assisi was situated.

Very quickly, we adapted to the situation, the world we were immediately in became the world that mattered to us personally, and the unattainable world outside lost interest very soon.

Before long different groups for study began to spring up. The great majority of chaps settled for 'industry'. Everyone set about making small, almost doll's house size, ovens and stoves for brewing-up and cooking the food from the Red Cross parcels, those heaven-sent life-savers. The cut-up empty tins were used for this and for making drinking mugs with strips of tin, made rigid, with wire rolled into the edges for the handles. Nothing was wasted. These tiny stoves made the most of the only fuel we had, little bits of wood chippings we managed to find, steal or even strip off our bunks.

Towards dusk every day, it was an extraordinary sight to see all these tiny stoves, down on the bare patch, twinkling away in the half-light and smoke pouring out of the chimneys. Grown men would be kneeling down, eyes blinded by the smoke, blowing to keep the fire alight, or using a flat piece of tin to fan or waft the flames. These fans soon became known as 'wafters'.

As soon as anyone completed their cooking or boiling, they would let out a call of 'Embers!' Then there would be a mad rush to get to them. The first chap there would then carefully tip the red hot remains of the stove into his own oven, and begin wafting and blowing for all he was worth! The smoke and the sparkling fires, with the crouching figures of men, form one of the lasting memories of the camp. It was quite awesomely beautiful at times, like a backcloth in one of the old Drury Lane musical spectaculars.

Brewing up during the day was a hazardous business, as no one knew when a snap roll call would be called and precious stove fuel would have to be abandoned, the warming-up food might be too hot to carry and would have to be left and might never be found again. I very soon had to face up to these irritating parades and accept the fact that 'irregularity' was now the 'regular' pattern of our lives.

As men got better and better at handling the broken-up empty tins from our food parcels, industry thrived. While more and more caught the bug, others moved on to quite advanced models with 'oven' doors, and little compartments to keep things warm while something else was being cooked. Even I tried my hand at it and made myself a useful drinking mug.

Imagine what it was like in those buildings all day. All the time there would be a constant tap, tap, tapping of stones hammering on tin, beating it into shape. At times it was sheer bedlam, at others like a shipyard, with a battleship being built!

At night, as my bunk was near the door — useful for fresh air, I hoped — there was the hazard of any of those 650 men, at any time of the night, having to nip out to the toilet. All of them, it seemed, wore at least their army boots, if nothing else, and clumped up to the big ten or twelve foot door cum gate, which apparently had to be allowed to slam shut each way, each time, as part of the ritual! Perhaps this was an assertion, psychologically, of what personal freedom of action was still left to them! The lights stayed on dimly all night but, wonderfully, I found the disability of being deaf in one ear became an 'asset' at last.

Every day, carrying out the discipline of starting with a quiet time, usually before folk woke up and began their tin-work or other activities, brought a great sense of achievement and satisfaction during the day, as I ticked off the job done, or the interview carried out. Many times I wondered how much longer this sense of thrill and interest, in the essentially restricted set of circumstances could last.

Of course, having been up in the desert with the army for so long had prepared us in some measure for the all-male society we were now in, but the feeling of not knowing how long this kind of life was likely to go on for was daunting, to say the least, and I was more than grateful for the continuing sense of purpose and form my life kept.

I found myself thinking how could I best help the others. There were so many of them. How could I make friends with, and keep the friendship of, my oh so close neighbours? Getting to know one man or a few men, as God directed, was the answer to my initial, overwhelming bewilderment.

At one stage there were over twenty of us meeting in the early morning in the winter in the cold, concrete concert hall, with no heating, just sitting on the bare concrete floor with our blankets round our shoulders, perhaps passing my pocket Bible round, perhaps praying, but above all being willing to find God's direction and plan for each of us for that day. It was a means of renewing the new-found faith which took away the worry and despair of the enforced separation of men and their families, and gaining in a new trust in God's provision and care for us all.

One strange thing, quite a few of these men, without any prompting from me at all, got the thought that they should stop smoking. This at a time when smoking could possibly have seemed to take off the keen edge of hunger, or perhaps relieved the stress of prison life.

12

The Drama Group

We were captured in June, but it was December before we got our first mail. I believe it was November before our families knew that we were no longer 'missing', but were in the comparative safety of a prisoner-of-war camp.

Sitting on my high bunk one day, peacefully viewing the world around me, a curious encounter took place. I suddenly noticed a strange, wild-eyed fellow standing staring at me. As I caught his eye, he looked quickly away. This went on for two or three days. It was disconcerting, to say the least. What had I done? I didn't know him! I began to be frightened of him.

I don't know whether Frank Buchman, the founder of MRA, coined the phrase or whether he was quoting someone, but I remembered hearing him say on one occasion: 'A nation's best defence is the love and gratitude of her neighbours.' I got the thought that perhaps the philosophy would work with *this* neighbour, so I determined, next time he turned up, to tackle him. Sure enough, along he came and started to watch me.

Not a little fearful, I climbed down from my bunk and went over to him. I probably told him my name, asked him his and where he came from, and then, the ice having been broken, the reason for his watchfulness came out. He'd noticed that I didn't smoke, so would I like to swap my issue of cigarettes for his sugar? Well, this *was* a turn up for the book! He was doing his nut for fags, and I certainly needed all the sugar I could get hold of to keep my strength up. So I found a benefactor, a shy friend and not an enemy at all!

One seemingly irrational thought I had was to start an art class. No paper, no pencils, one would have thought no possibility, but our need was met with a fly leaf from this or that book, the odd pencils from here and there. Then my notice on the camp notice board got a sizeable class together.

I soon found that there was no question of my being the teacher or the expert. Very quickly, I was being taught myself by my 'pupils'. There were some most talented artists among us, who were only too keen to pass on such tips as how to create a sense of distance and perspective.

My next inspiration was to put on a play. I'd done a lot of amateur dramatics in my time. I'd started the Paludian Players for my old school when I'd left, and acted with a couple of other local companies. When I went to work in London, I joined an English evening class, and was roped in to its offshoot, The Childerley Players, a repertory company which performed for old peoples' homes, for clubs and guilds. We used to enter the 'Stewart Headlam' Shakespeare competition every year, and as finalists we would have a gala evening with the other area winners at the George Vth Theatre, the Scala, and once we even did our scene from *Macbeth* at the Old Vic itself. With all this experience behind me I thought we ought to be able to get a drama group going.

As I'd always disliked the discipline of learning words, and as we hadn't any scripts here, we could all make it up as we went. Amazingly, although I found enough volunteers, they all insisted on having their parts written down so they *could* learn them. By all means talk it out first, get the dialogue, but it *must* be written out and laboriously learnt!

I discovered a very strange thing. Out of all the one-act plays I'd been in, let alone seen, although I could remember the plots I couldn't for the life of me remember how they ended. Then I thought of two plays, the first was *The Monkey's Paw* by W. W. Jacobs. It was a play dealing with the dangers of being discontented with things as they are, of being greedy and of making demands. I would play the Father, a sergeant would play the Mother, a very dramatic role this, and another fellow the third part.

Unfortunately, the 'Mother' fell ill, and we all had to switch. I had to do the mother part, which I had wanted to do in the first place, but I'd decided it would be selfish to grab it. This was a really meaty role, with scenes of hysterical frenzy, and the melodramatic collapse in the open doorway on a darkened stage, with moonlight pouring in as I slowly sank to the floor. So, with dressing-gown/overcoat now disguised as a skirt, and a sisal string wig, I had my big moment! The whole play went like a bomb and, to mix metaphors a bit, you could hear a pin drop.

After this first success we moved on to the only other plot I could remember, that of Dickens's *Christmas Carol*. What he would have thought of our dialogue, I shudder to think! The Methodist padre played Bob Cratchit, the ghosts of Christmasses Past, Present and Future, were played by the C of E man, the R C chaplain and my Orthodox Jewish friend. Quite an ecumenical effort. I played Scrooge.

This time my dressing gown played itself, my long johns served as tights cum trousers, and an improvised nightcap completed the wardrobe. There I was, centre stage, ad-libbing away to my heart's content. At first being mean, greedy, selfish and all the bad things, next getting a conviction of sin, deciding to change, and then making restitution. In my soliloquies, and in my asides, I was able to make sure that the audience realised that *we* all needed to do this, and that we could start now! This play we were asked to repeat for the POWs in the camp hospital. (Talk about a 'captive' audience!) As it was nearly Christmas Day, it all went down well, including the jug of water on the heads of the carol singers off stage!

On Christmas Eve I received my first letter from home. It was from my sister, a momentous event. On top of this not only was it my turn to receive a British Red Cross parcel, but also a Canadian parcel. These occasional extra parcels from Canada actually had milk chocolate and real butter in them. The Roman Catholics had a very nice crib and a set of figures, and laid on a Midnight Mass, with the crib, which had been lent them by the Italians, as a great feature.

That Christmas was one of the happiest Christmases of my life, if not the happiest. Having nothing, everything was added to me. The excitement and joy from the gifts of the letter and two parcels, and to top it all the celebration of Mass, were indescribable. I was awake all night with the sheer wonder of it!

13

My Name is Called Out!

I always tried to keep my record straight. If I did anything, or said anything, wrong, I would get conviction about it in my early time of quiet the next morning, and then I would put it right as soon as I could. For instance, one evening we were suddenly told there would be a bonus issue of boiling water for brewing-up. Falling for specious arguments in my mind, I took along my spare mug, mumbled something about a mate might need it, and accepted a second helping. No one else, I hoped, would want it and I would be sitting pretty! As it happened, no one did need it, but nor did I! One mug was plenty.

I had to put this right, so I went to see the dispensing sergeant the next day and confessed my greed, and also, to put it mildly, my muddled, covetous thinking. I had no idea whether I would be punished, but my pride certainly took a beating. Fortunately for me, the sergeant understood and overlooked the rather murky episode.

Perhaps the routine of camp life had begun to give an illusion of security, for gradually people began to slip into a much more materialistic way of living. Bingo began, 'Housey, housey!' as it was called in the army, and as the one time that we could depend on not being interrupted by snap roll calls was the time of the Sunday morning services, the clash of interests between gambling and any kind of corporate worship soon became very real.

The organisers began to get rich on the currency, mostly cigarettes, and a kind of gangsterism began to develop. As in civilian prisons, 'Tobacco Barons' emerged, each with his coterie of henchmen to collect debts, etc. I remember seeing one of these types sitting on his bunk, ordering one of his helpers to go and get him a tin of meat and giving him a handful of cigarettes to barter with. One wondered whether bullying or intimidation would be the next step.

An Anglican bishop, a New Zealander as it happened, was allowed out on parole to go round the camps taking confirmation services. He came to ours and our prepared candidates were duly confirmed. So far, so good. Then he went a step further. He apparently ordered our C of E man to have distinct and separated-off services, and no longer join with the Methodist padre in the combined sort of service we had been having. I couldn't see the necessity of this division. I felt that this was a time when men wanted a faith, not a *form* of religion.

After the bishop had gone, the chaplain told us of his resolve to obey orders, to separate off and have a full C of E service, and nothing the Methodist padre and I could say would shake him.

As the Sunday approached, the Methodist padre and I met and prayed together that even now this division would be prevented, or if it did take place, it would not weaken men's faith. Sunday morning came and with it the news that our C of E man had been taken ill and was in hospital suffering from some kind of paralysis of the legs. The Methodist man not only very sportingly carried on with a combined service, but performed the full Church of England communion service for those who wanted it.

We heard later that the sick chaplain was repatriated to England, and that as he arrived his illness left him and he was able to walk again. Was it the stress that caused the paralysis? Or our prayers? Or God's way of preserving unity? He was a very nice young man, but as a C of E man myself, albeit newly confirmed, I didn't really see the importance of emphasising our Protestant diversity.

I've told you of my occasional forays with my sergeant friend, 'Griff'. One day an announcement was made that all holders of the Geneva Convention Red Cross 'Protected Personnel' cards should hand them in to the office. I'm afraid I didn't bother.

My card had been issued to me under such strange circumstances in Tobruk hospital, that although I had been doing 'Protected Personnel' duties in the Ambulance Car Company, and later medical duties in the hospital, I felt that as I was actually in the RASC, and in fact carried a rifle (I suppose in case we were ever transferred to a military unit), the card didn't really apply to me. Now this is where 'Griff' comes in. We had had one of our rows about nothing. I can remember getting the conviction for two or three days that I should apologize once again to him. I fought against this, feeling that I'd apologized too many times, let him approach me first, and so on.

At last I decided to look him up and say I was sorry. He explained that his stomach was all upset and it made him irritable, I was not to take any notice, and he was sorry also. Then, quite out of the blue, he asked me if I'd handed in my Red Cross card? I said no, and told him my reasons. He got very firm with me and said I must hand it in. It was an order. So, rather regretfully (it was a reassuring feeling having the card making me, however tenuously, 'Protected Personnel'), I dutifully handed it in and forgot all about it.

A fortnight later, a string of names was called out on parade for repatriation and *my* name was one of them! There was to be an exchange of prisoners. I couldn't believe my ears when I heard it. Could it be true? Would it actually happen? My cup, to put it mildly, was overflowing. This was the miracle to end all miracles!

One thing marred my great joy, there was a YMCA man in the camp I was friendly with, an Irishman, and he of course was a natural, non-combatant candidate for repatriation, but had not been selected. Why me? Why not him? He wrote a book later, and so deep did the fancied hurt sink in that he went so far as to suggest I'd fiddled the card!

14

The Way Back

On the first leg of our journey back home, we were on the train heading for a transit camp and I did my first trade with the enemy. On the train I had with me a tin of cocoa, but no bread. As there was no possibility of any hot water on the train, I swapped the tin for a large bread roll, with one of the guards.

We were put on better rations almost immediately at the transit camp and began to put on a little weight and fatten up a bit. We stayed here for four or five weeks, I believe, improving in health all the while, but still very much under weight and still not quite sure of our good fortune.

At last we were put on to a hospital ship and set sail for the neutral port of Smyrna. There for all the world to see was a waiting British hospital ship flying the Union Jack. What a series of terrific emotional climaxes: Christmas, the calling out of my name on parade, and now this superb sight!

To crown everything, I saw a turtle swimming in the sea. This was the first zoo animal I'd ever seen in its natural habitat, apart from a few deer and, or course, desert rats — and the dolphins which had followed our troopship at times on the way out to the Middle East.

After a super welcome and a lot of kindly fussing and caring, we settled in to our cabins, with their bunks and clean sheets and pillows, and prepared for a 'Mediterranean Cruise' over to Alexandria.

Back in Alexandria, we immediately felt a sense of anti-climax. Everything was just the same as when we left it. No one knew we were back. No one knew we had been away, or cared, come to that. They all had their day-to-day problems to get on with, with none of the compensating 'excitement', if you could call it that, of being where the action was. We began to feel that we were no longer special.

We were quickly entrained for Cairo and moved into the long established RAMC barracks there, with its Country Club atmosphere and appearance. We received a most dreadful, unfriendly welcome from the resident CSM, which was almost comical in its brutal frankness. He had us on parade and proceeded to tell us we were dirty. This was probably indisputable, although by comparison we were beginning to feel quite clean again, and probably indisciplined. He confined us to barracks until we were issued with regulation new khaki.

The issue happened quickly enough for the Medical Corps types among us who, in a sense, belonged there, but we in the RASC were to wait until we were sent to our own camp at Quassassin. Impatient as we quite naturally were to taste 'freedom', now we'd got it, some of us got round the ban by getting mates to buy us bush shirts and shorts in town and scrounging South African brown shoes and so on, and got past the guards on the gate that way.

A rather amazing coincidence happened in this camp, or rather barracks. In the reading room I found a back number of a quite reputable, glossy, illustrated weekly from England, with pictures in it taken from a film we had co-operated in making, up in the desert, before we were captured, of an RASC Ambulance Car Company, in action and convoy.

Alas! according to the captions under the pictures, we were all the brave boys of the Royal Army *Medical* Corps in action under shellfire. The realistic smoke seen drifting over the ambulances (in much closer formation than the regulation distance in order to make a decent picture), was from a stack of old tyres I'd made into a bonfire, stage right so to speak, to add to the realism. The wounded soldier bravely giving a 'thumbs up' through the window of one ambulance was our lance-corporal, with a red ink-stained bandaged arm in a sling!

The caption under one picture even made us into a forward dressing station, with what was supposed to be an emergency operation being carried out on a table.

After interminable hanging around, we were finally sent off to our own camp on the Canal, near Ismailia. So, another step nearer home! Here the situation was a bit better. After all, it was our own corp, we did belong, so to speak, and I believe there was actually a remark of welcome on one parade. I suspect we were more of a passing, but rather irritating, interruption of the routine.

I heard from England that a friend of mine was in the next camp just down the road, so one morning I set out, before the heat of the day got really going, and went to look him up. Reaching the camp, I saw there had just been a parade, but the parade ground was deserted except for a group of four or five NCOs standing in the middle chatting.

Completely forgetting all about the 'sanctity' of the 'Barrack Square', I walked over to them. At one time I had cultivated what I'd fondly hoped was a 'fratefully refaned', 'county' accent. My friends had teased me out of this false front, and I had resumed a more middle-of-the-road speaking voice.

In times of stress, however, I used unconsciously to stick it on again. This was one of those occasions! The group on the parade ground turned out to be composed almost entirely of company sergeant-majors and regimental sergeant-majors. Coupled with this, I suddenly remembered I shouldn't be on the 'square' at all! (Barrack squares are banned for all ordinary mortals, except for parades.)

In my nervousness, determined not to panic, I stuck on my best and countiest voice and blurted out, 'Excuse me, could you tell me where the "such and such" regiment is quartered?' To my horror, they all turned smartly round, stamped to attention and one of them swung a magnificent salute to me!

Why they didn't eat me alive, I don't know. I pretended not to notice, and looked every way but at them, and one of them gave me the information I wanted. I resisted the temptation to turn and run for it, thanked them and marched off as smartly as I could. Perhaps their surprise saved me!

While I was in this camp waiting for repatriation to England, I volunteered to help the padre in his tent/church, as a server, in the daily, early morning communion service. He was a strange man. He never spoke, except to explain what he wanted done, and how: this book here, the cross over there, and so on. No one seemed to come to these services, so it was just the padre and I on our own.

He only unbent once. He came along to the NAAFI one evening to drum up some enthusiasm for a concert of light classical music on records. This should make a welcome change from the usual evenings we had in camp. Of course, he explained, we should have to behave properly: no tapping of feet to the beat of the music, or conducting with one's hands, even nodding in time could be annoying to the person sitting behind.

In spite of these patronising and ominous warnings, quite a bunch turned up including, of course, the padre. He, strangely enough, was the one to offend. Every so often during the playing of the music, he would stuff his pipe and light up. This usually took three or four matches, and as he didn't blow them out but waved them in the air to extinguish them (all part of his ritual of contentment), we were treated to a kind of Handel's *Water Music* with the fireworks thrown in!

I had made friends with another sergeant on the way back from Italy, but in spite of the natural separations due to rank as I was only a driver, we got together after hours, and would sometimes go into Ismailia, on our time off.

One day, we decided to go in early, for the whole day. So we got out all our best gear, which we had bought in Cairo, polished up our brown South African shoes, put on our sunglasses and the coloured 'General Montgomery' silk cravats and set off for the bus. Suddenly, we heard a loud voice: 'Hey, you there!' Could he mean us? We hadn't much time, the bus might go. 'Just a minute!' he called. I think he was a captain. Anyway, we thought we'd better go over.

'Who do you think you are?' he said to me. So I told him: 'Driver Walter, 228136, *Sir*!'

'Who do you think you are?' he repeated. I repeated my answer, adding deprecatingly, but hopefully playing a trump card, that we were two of the returned POWs and we were just off on a day pass to Ismailia.

'I know who you are!' he thundered, 'get those things off. Who do you think you are?' By this time, we were nearly bursting with laughter. We dare not say anything, so we saluted and hurried to change into our regulation kit.

Well, admittedly, our bush shirts weren't quite the right khaki, but they actually fitted us, and we were wearing officer-type shoes and coloured scarves, but we had felt that a bit of flamboyant dressing-up was understandable after the awful Hungarian cast-offs we'd had to wear in PG 70.

The officer was a stickler for the regulations and so we hurried back to our billets and changed into our ill-fitting Regular Army issue, and caught a later bus.

A few days later, I was off for Ismailia, this time on my own, and fondly thinking that lightning doesn't strike in the same place twice, put on all my 'best' clothes. I was just passing the officers' mess on my way to the bus, when the familiar voice rang out:

'Hey there! Who do you think you are?' Well, I thought, by this time, even he should know who I am. Anyway, I answered him patiently, and explained all about the regulation kit not fitting and so on, but not to be outdone, he then sent me over to the quartermaster's stores, and to say he'd sent me, for another lot of, unfortunately, still typically, ill-fitting uniform. To make matters worse, it was in my own time!

The QM gave me a funny look but said nothing, and soon I was on my way to the famous 'Blue Kettle' YMCA services club beside the lake in Ismailia, where I tried to imagine I was a free, civilised and independent gentleman for a brief while, with a perfect right to be alive!

15

On Convalescent Leave

At our base camp, we met up with quite a few of the personnel and NCOs from our training battalion in England. This seemed like poetic justice to us. We had been 'less than the dust', just ignorant 'civvies', who had to have our bad 'civvy' driving habits corrected, who had to be licked into shape, and forced into a military mould. There were quite a lot of these Regular Army fellows who loved enforcing the pettifogging and sometimes downright demoralising methods of making a diverse mob of all types of men into a unified, unquestioning, undemanding, mobile mass, to become a part of the whole British Army!

Here were the men who, from their comfortable safe jobs at the training barracks, were drafted out at last, with no overseas experience, no sunburn, looking pale, still to 'get their knees brown'. Not really knowing where they were, or where they were going, stripped of all their implied superiority as instructors, and here were we, the one-time helpless putty in their hands, now, with all the experiences which had been thrust upon us, having 'beaten' the Desert, been part of the front line, and been POWs, it was difficult for us not to feel superior in our turn!

Gradually, as time went on, our ex-POW novelty wore off, and we began to be treated as ordinary soldiers, but first we were sent up to Nathanya by the sea, to recuperate. This was a lovely spot in Palestine with red cliffs and the sparkling blue Mediterranean. Perhaps it was intended as a small compensation for all the privations we'd had to put up with, although I think most of us would rather have been shipped straight home.

It was at Nathanya that I witnessed a rare astronomical occurrence, the re-orientation of a star, I believe it is called. One evening I was on my way to the camp theatre when I happened to look up at the sky over the sea. It was not quite dark, and there was a three-quarter moon without a cloud in sight and unusually near it was a really bright star. Happening to look up again, about ten minutes later, I found the star had moved even closer. Gradually, it reached the stage when the star seemed to be on the actual edge of the dark part of the moon, like a great diamond ring in the sky.

I'd never heard of this phenomenon before and you can imagine my amazement when the star disappeared and then re-appeared from behind the moon, this time on the bright side. I found it very exciting, although I must say the other chaps took it all in their stride, and didn't seem particularly interested. I suppose we were all in such a state of uncertainty about our repatriation and impatient to get cracking on our return journey to England, home and beauty.

The fact that we were due to go home seemed too good to be true, and we still feared the great

British Army in its soulless way might decide to bend the Geneva Convention rules and find a way of keeping us out there in the Middle East, even on non-military jobs, instead of repatriating us.

The camp at Nathanya was staffed by Italian POWs who were allowed a great deal of liberty in the evenings and fraternisation was the order of the day. I remember being in a tent with a bunch of them one evening, eager to hear from someone who had so recently been in their homeland.

Hoping to point out to them how lucky they were to be *our* prisoners, I told them of our dreadful conditions and of the dirt, disease and shortage of food in the Italian prison camps. To my surprise, they matched all my stories of privation and discomfort with their own stories with them as the victims and us as the captors. I guess that in a war you don't go into battle having prepared living quarters and hot meals for thousands of possible prisoners!

Not to be outdone by this counter-propaganda, I proceeded to inform them that *we* had been exchanged at the rate of seven Italians to one Englishman! This was too much for them, and the hitherto friendly atmosphere of yarn-swapping was, not surprisingly, quite electrifyingly snapped. They all got up as one man, and stalked out!

Of course, it was the ratio of prisoners that had been captured by us, and which it was more convenient to send back, rather than an assessment of man-to-man value, but I'm afraid they took it the wrong way. They were furious! It was wrong, and, to put it mildly, undiplomatic, of me to say it, but these particular prisoners had landed themselves such a cushy job and were having it so good in quite literally a 'holiday camp' imprisonment that I couldn't resist it.

After our convalescence we very quickly sank back into being part of the herd. The actual heat and discomfort on troop trains were so great, that they almost wiped out the benefits of our seaside holiday.

Eventually the rumours hotted up into facts, and we joined a ship going back to England from Alexandria. The only clear memory I have of this time is of our train journey from our canal base to Ismailia and the sight of big groups of storks foregathering in the desert, quite near the train, getting ready for their great annual get-together for the mass migration. Later, we saw a vast inverted funnel of these birds slowly circling and soaring way up into the clear blue sky. There were thousands of them going through their pre-migratory ritual. Perhaps they were just flexing their muscles prior to take-off for Europe, or wherever storks go. It was quite awe-inspiring.

Our ship was able to come back through the Mediterranean but it seemed to us, impatient as we were to get home, that it meandered quite meaninglessly. There were long, interminable, seemingly pointless delays outside various very interesting looking ports, Algiers and Gibraltar among them, but we were not allowed to go ashore.

We were never told why we stopped and waited. It might have helped if we had known. Perhaps we were waiting for the odd U-boat to leave our route, or even to have one removed. We never knew. We just felt we were being messed about, and all we could do was try to develop the social side of life on board ship and take a keen, if distant, interest in the places as we passed them, places we'd heard about all our lives. The sight of the 'Rock' was very impressive, and we had to fight hard against the feelings of frustration at being so near and yet so far. After two or three days lingering offshore, even its great size began to pall.

16

Despatch Rider

Back to England at last, but this part is all very confused, perhaps by the excitement. Fortunately, it was a dry, warm, lovely autumn and this helped our adjustment, climatically anyway!

First I contacted my sister, who lived in Walton-on-Thames. She gave me a very warm, emotional welcome. Then over to Ruislip in Middlesex to greet my brother and his family. After a tentative posting to a place in Kent, I was finally attached to a transport unit at the White City, Shepherd's Bush. This was convenient in many ways.

I drove my first big lorry at this depot. It was a 3-tonner, big to me, anyway. We used to go out two or three at a time to pick up provisions from the most out-of-the-way and inaccessible warehouses and then deliver them to different barracks in various parts of London.

It was wrongly assumed that I was used to driving this big stuff, and, without a try-out, I was put on an early morning run with two others. It was half dark and thick fog, and by the time we'd reached the end of Wood Lane I was at the rear out of touch, sight and sound of the others. As I had been given no address to go to, but was told, simply, to follow the others, I felt the strain somewhat! However, the others waited for me at Shepherd's Bush and we re-grouped successfully.

The maintenance and cleaning of this huge lorry was the next nightmare. However, I remembered that if you really put your heart into it, any job can become interesting and rewarding. So I took on my lorry and found, in this way, that I quite enjoyed the Herculean task. In fact, I did it so successfully, I won the prize for the best kept vehicle, for two weeks running. Perhaps it was on the strength of this performance that I was promoted to the astronomical rank of lance-corporal!

About this time I was sent up the HQ of the Royal Army Service Corps, to act as despatch rider. This suited me fine. I liked being my own master on the despatch rides able, to a certain extent, to work out my own speed and the route I followed for my scheduled run. Later on, when back with my unit, on convoy work, I rather assumed authority at traffic control on crossroads and so on.

A sergeant, who also lived in the same empty house which we used as our billet, made a decision to let God run his life. He was a Roman Catholic and one of his first decisions was to return to his Church. The priest he saw immediately harnessed his re-born enthusiasm and got him contributing articles to a publication on the evangelical side of the Church's work, *The Sword of the Spirit*. I don't know what the circulation figures were, but apparently it had quite an effective outreach.

At lunchtime, one day, the colonel sent for me, and told me a convoy had left Epping for Shepherd's Bush two days before, but had not turned up and had completely disappeared. I was ordered to go and look for it. I'd had the thought that morning that I should go along to a home in Charles Street, used as a centre for MRA, and shift stores during my afternoon spare time. This new order was a complication.

I asked God what to do. The thought came: 'Go to Charles Street and tell of the change of plan, then go to Notting Hill High Street.' This I did quite quickly and there, sure enough, was the convoy, ambling along with all the time in the world! What had happened to them, or where they'd been, I never found out, but I got them to their destination and returned to HQ in Knightsbridge.

As soon as I got back, the colonel sent for me. Leaning across his desk and pointing a finger at me, he demanded, 'How did you find the convoy so quickly?' I told him how I tried to let God run my life and had sought His guidance, obeyed the thoughts that came — and there was the convoy! He didn't say anything for a moment, but gave me rather a funny look, then dismissed me, thanking me.

Lessons were learnt the hard way on the motorbike. If I'd compromised in my living or thinking even, my confidence was broken and I drove badly. There were wet wooden block roads to skid on, frozen patches to slip on and, on some routes, tram lines to throw me. I certainly needed God's protection.

Sometimes on my route I'd see doodlebugs on the skyline landing in a big ring round me, visible for miles around from the vantage point of a hilltop on the road. Some, of course, were nearer to the barracks. This would be usually at night time, a potentially more frightening time, I suppose, although I must admit I was always more frightened of the NCOs, than I ever was of bombs or shelling. I was absolutely confident that God was going to bring me through safe and sound. The roads I took on my despatch run each day changed over night, in appearance, with this rain of bombs.

On one occasion, I'd just found out there was a speed limit in Hyde Park and I decided that I would try to stick to it in future but, on this particular day, there was someone en route I wanted to call on. If I obeyed this speed limit, I'd be running my schedule a bit close.

The thought came, 'Never mind the speed limit, get a move on, and fit in your quick visit.' I obeyed, and just as I left the park and reached the other side of the Cumberland Hotel, the last but one V2 landed at Speaker's Corner, by Marble Arch, just about where I'd have reached if I'd not had the thought to speed things up through the park!

Whenever the weather got too bad with fog or snow on the evening run in the black-out, the officer in charge would often suggest posting the 'Standing Orders' for the next day. Later, I had the opportunity to suggest that it would save quite a lot of fuel if we did this every day, regardless of the weather.

I don't know whether it was a result of my suggestion, but very soon, I found myself a 'redundant' despatch rider at HQ. Back I want to the White City barracks and on to various courses: to Salisbury Plain for a poison gas protection course, and another to

Preston for an English course, I think the Army had begun to think in terms of 'further education' for the men in the forces.

While I was at Salisbury on the gas course, I saw gliders filled with Second Front men being towed to France. That was the first we heard that we had landed in Europe. It was awesome and rather creepy, seeing these great planes flying very low coming over the brow of the hill, and then the gliders, on long tow ropes, way behind, quite silent.

The V2s were the opposite to the doodle-bug bombs, the V1s. The bugs travelled comparatively slowly, could be seen and heard and were sometimes shot down by pursuing aircraft. The V2s were heard as they landed, but the sound of their coming came after the explosion, they were so fast!

One of my duties as a DR was escorting guns and ammunition to the south coast, hot foot, to try and intercept the doodle-bugs. On our way, the sight of these fire-belching, small plane-like bombs, seven or eight at a time, coming in over the hills in Kent was strangely exciting. At last we could see point and purpose in our work. This was direct participation.

This particular convoy work was so obviously of vital importance that I had no qualms whatever at holding up traffic at road junctions, and keeping the trucks with their cargoes constantly and steadily moving down to their new bases. It was worth putting up with the abuse and unconcealed fury of the held-up bus drivers, taxis and other traffic. The priority was clear to me, and would have been to them, had they known of our mission. Then, possibly, at the end of the long return journey, to be greeted with the blackout, perhaps rain, with wet cobble stones and tramlines, was physically and emotionally the last straw! Quite terrifying.

The acute sense of need and protection which I had is not unique to my experience, I feel sure.

17

De-Mob 'Daze'

I was in London for VE Day. I was able to get a seat on the wall surrounding the vast space around the Victoria monument outside Buckingham Palace. Many people had spent the night out there to get a good view of the King and Queen. Being agile and reasonable enterprising, I found an old piece of fencing and using this as a makeshift ladder I was able to shin up and find myself a place with a grandstand view. What a day that was!

The next great excitement began to loom ahead. De-mob dates started to appear on the notice board. You could almost work out which group you would be in, almost which day! Then the great day arrived, and with it a strange anti-climax. There was no one around in the barracks to say goodbye to, I had no family home to go to, there was no ceremony of dismissal, let alone of being discharged, just a trip to Olympia with a group of chaps I did not know to pick up my issue of 'civvy' clothes. There I was, alone in a milling throng of strangers, all of whom seemed to be hurrying for trains and buses, their one thought to get home.

Coming out of the army after such a traumatic and drastic time during the war was quite a bit like coming out of prison camp: a terrific experience, but quite personal to you, and lonely. Everyone had their own personal 'prisons' to escape from, and no one could share this moment with you.

I had, at last, complete freedom to do what God wanted me to do. What *I* wanted? What God wanted for me would be the unqualified best thing, that was certain. During the first years in camps I'd always said that after the outdoor life in the army, I'd never go back to working indoors again, but now the moment had come, I really felt that I'd had enough fresh air.

My home town and display work called me, and so in 1945 I rejoined my old firm in Slough. The prolonged break in the army had given me renewed zest. I was ready for the challenges of 'civvy street'. Something new and exciting was going to emerge from the emotional stress and turmoil of the last years.

In war, you could see the enemy and the problems, and the fight to survive. I was equipped now with the experience of God's direction in the most hair-raising situations. This was my armoury with which to face peace.

The years since have been momentous. The quiet insistent voice within has been guiding me on the job, in my marriage and in the all-out effort to build a world that really works — a world where the needs of friends and neighbours for a meaning and purpose are met by a loving God.

But that is another story.